I HAVE MY MOTHER'S EYES

vo dopisano żony
w oślicl. Ur Semul.

I HAVE MY MOTHER'S EYES

A HOLOCAUST MEMOIR ACROSS GENERATIONS

Barbara Ruth Bluman

RONSDALE PRESS &
VANCOUVER HOLOCAUST EDUCATION SOCIETY

I HAVE MY MOTHER'S EYES
Copyright © 2009 Barbara Ruth Bluman

RONSDALE PRESS
3350 West 21st Avenue, Vancouver, B.C., Canada V6S 1G7
www.ronsdalepress.com

Typesetting: Julie Cochrane, in Granjon 11.5 pt on 16
Cover Design: Shawna Romain & Kazuko Kusumoto
Paper: Ancient Forest Friendly "Silva" (FSC) — 100% post-consumer waste,
   totally chlorine-free and acid-free

Ronsdale Press wishes to thank the following for their support of its publishing program: the Canada Council for the Arts, the Government of Canada through the Book Publishing Industry Development Program (BPIDP), the British Columbia Arts Council and the Province of British Columbia through the British Columbia Book Publishing Tax Credit program.

Library and Archives Canada Cataloguing in Publication

Bluman, Barbara R
   I have my mother's eyes: a holocaust memoir across generations / Barbara Ruth Bluman.

Co-published by the Vancouver Holocaust Education Centre.
ISBN 978-1-55380-070-5

   1. Bluman, Susan. 2. Holocaust, Jewish (1939–1945) — Poland. 3. World War, 1939–1945 — Jews — Poland — Biography. 4. Jews — Poland — Biography. 5. Bluman, Barbara R. — Health. 6. Cancer — Patients — Canada — Biography. 7. Mothers and daughters — Biography. 1. Vancouver Holocaust Education Centre 11. Title.

DS134.72.B58 B58 2009   940.53'18092   C2009-900660-X

At Ronsdale Press we are committed to protecting the environment. To this end we are working with Markets Initiative (www.oldgrowthfree.com) and printers to phase out our use of paper produced from ancient forests. This book is one step towards that goal.

Printed in Canada by Marquis Printing, Quebec

Foreword

MY MOTHER, BARBARA RUTH BLUMAN, began the task of recounting her mother's escape during the Holocaust from Nazi-occupied Poland. This was no small assignment and made all the more challenging by her cancer diagnosis. When she died in 2001, the narrative was not yet complete; she asked me to finish it for her. As the initial pain of my mother's death began to settle, I undertook the process of completing her legacy.

The inspiration to publish this book began with the realization that my grandmother and mother's stories needed to be shared beyond our family circle. The Wosk Publishing Program of the Vancouver Holocaust Education Centre (VHEC) provided the opportunity to do so. I am grateful to the VHEC for seeing the value in this book and for their ongoing commitment to Holocaust education and understanding.

To complete my mother's work, I relied on the assistance of many. My cousin Adam Lewis Schroeder bravely tackled the first editing phase of the manuscript. In the midst of his own busy writing career and raising a family, Adam took the time to reorganize the memoir and even managed to interview my grandmother not long before she died in order to obtain a few last details.

I want to acknowledge the whole publishing team at Ronsdale Press for all the work they have done to bring this book to fruition. In particular, I want to thank Colin Thomas, who edited my grandmother's story and invested countless hours in helping me reshape the existing material in my mother's story. Through interviews with various family members and friends we were able to piece together the hidden layers of my mother's experience and bring them to life. Thank you.

I would also like to acknowledge all of the people who shared their memories in order to bring our family's history to life in the most truthful way possible. Specifically, I would like to thank my Uncle George for being such an important resource, and my father Drew Schroeder, my uncle Bob Bluman and my friend Jim Henning for being willing to be interviewed.

I am grateful to my brothers, Michael and Sam, and my husband Marc, who supported me throughout this process and who were always willing to ease my insecurities and celebrate my accomplishments.

One final and important acknowledgement: I thank my mother Barbara Ruth Bluman, who trusted me far more than I have ever trusted myself to complete this book for her. Without her faith in me, I would never have had the courage to go deeper into our family story and truly learn what it means to have my mother's eyes.

Danielle Bluman Low (Schroeder)

January 2009

Hoffenberg Family Tree

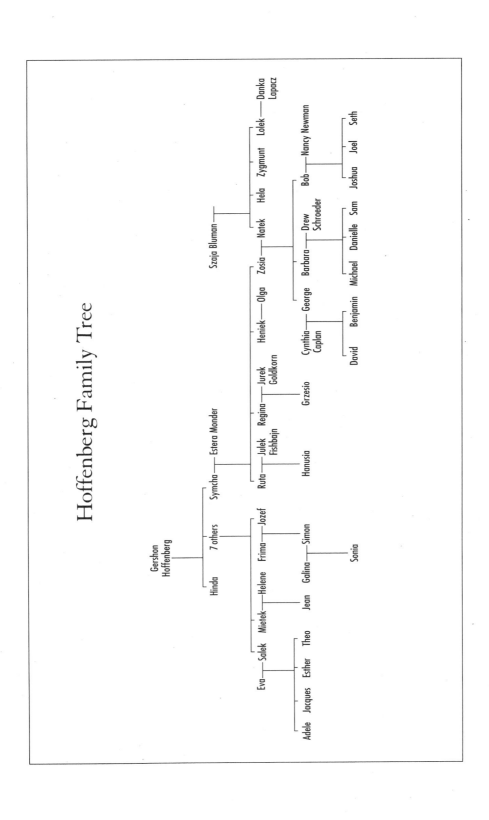

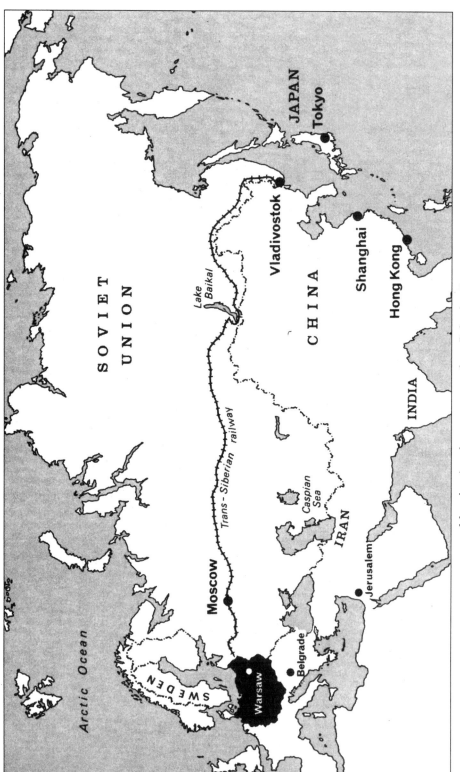

Map showing the escape route from Poland to Japan

I

Pieces of a Tea Set

ALL CHILDREN LOVE to hear about when they were babies. "Your eyes were so blue," her parents would tell her, "and so intelligent."

Six-year-old Zosia's colouring came from her father. He, too, had dark, curly hair — as well as the full beard of orthodox Jewish men — and his blue eyes were so clear that they were almost hypnotic.

Soon she would be too old for it, but Zosia still slept with her parents, Symcha and Estera Hoffenberg. Every night Symcha plied her with kisses, and then she nested in the contours of his body. When he took her shopping, she could cajole him into buying anything she wanted. They played cards together. And they walked. Even now, in the winter, the pair bundled up and walked through parks, along bustling streets, and over to the cinema to watch American movies made by Charlie Chaplin. In one, the poor little tramp was so hungry that he had to eat the nails from his shoes. Zosia loved the movies, but Symcha would always fall asleep, snoring and embarrassing his daughter. "It was worth every penny," he'd say as they made their way home. "I had my best sleep ever!"

The whole family attended services in the synagogue. Men and women sat apart, but sometimes Zosia was able to sneak over to the men's side and sit by her father. Symcha always seemed happy to see her, but he was too engrossed in prayers to give her much attention. His body swayed to the rhythm of the words as he chanted and prayed, and Zosia watched tears drip from his eyes.

Zosia's relationship with her mother was less easy. When Zosia was born on September 1, 1920, in Warsaw, Poland, Estera was thirty-nine years old and she already had three children: thirteen-year-old Ruta, ten-year-old Regina and nine-year-old Heniek, the only boy. Estera had been enjoying increased freedom as her children grew older, and she hadn't relished looking after a new baby.

Unlike her youngest daughter's bold, bright-eyed looks, Estera's features were dark and delicate. She was proud of her good figure and disapproved of women whom she felt did not look after themselves. Estera wore her long, dark hair in a neat, fashionable bun, and not a morning passed that she didn't put on her corset. Her days were often filled with appointments at the hairdresser, manicurist and dressmaker.

Symcha and Estera had been introduced by a matchmaker and, financially, it had proved to be a good match for the bride. Prior to the First World War, Poland was occupied by the Russians, and Zosia's maternal grandfather had run a thriving business selling medals and ornaments to the Russian soldiers. After the war, however, Poland regained its independence and, with the Russians' departure, Grandfather Monder lost the market for his medals. The store closed and he was left with boxes of useless merchandise.

Zosia loved her *dziadek*. Her grandfather still lived in the same large, gracious apartment that he had occupied when his business was lucrative, and every Saturday afternoon Zosia and her family would visit him. They always went on foot because devout Jews were prohibited from riding buses on the Sabbath. The walk seemed to take forever, and Zosia complained bitterly all the way, but her mood changed as soon as her smiling grandfather opened the door and wrapped her in his arms. She would play all afternoon with a box of his old medals — no toy could be more lovely or glamorous — and, when they were about to leave, he always selected a piece from a gold-plated tea set for her to take home and add to her collection.

Because Estera was the only one of Dziadek Moder's children to have married well, she and her husband were obliged to assist her family financially. Symcha did not assume this responsibility happily and Zosia hated to hear him complaining, "They always want money, money, and more money!" he would say. One day, when Zosia could stand it no longer, she took her small savings and handed them to her mother. "Please give these coins to Dziadek," she pleaded.

Symcha was very close to his brothers, with whom he ran a business called Bracia Hoffenberg, or Brothers Hoffenberg. It was a men's clothing store that sold garments produced by Jewish tailors who lived in Jewish villages, *shtetls*. Throughout Warsaw, the Hoffenberg name was associated with men's clothing, and the business was so profitable that Bracia Hoffenberg had acquired a significant portfolio of real estate. They were also in the fur business and had a contract with the Polish government to supply fur coats to railroad employees.

Symcha had the charm necessary to cajole the government officials. On Sundays, Zosia sometimes saw her father take strange men into his study. This was his private domain, with a big mahogany desk and an elaborate cabinet stocked with wine and hard liquor. The maid would take in a fresh bottle of vodka and close the door on her way out.

Symcha was one of nine children. Because the family was so large, there was a wide range in age between siblings, and Symcha's eldest sister Hinda had been married off to their father's youngest brother, their uncle. The youngest of Hinda's four sons was mentally challenged, and everyone attributed this to the inbreeding.

Zosia and her family lived on Swietokrzyska Street, half a block away from the elegant apartment building that housed Bracia Hoffenberg on its main floor. Symcha's father, Gershon Hoffenberg, lived in the building, and so did Symcha's brothers and their families. All told, Zosia's father and her uncles had fourteen children, who spent so much time together they seemed like siblings.

Because Zosia and her sisters were the only girl cousins, they received much attention from the boys. The male cousins were all obliged to work downstairs at the store, although none of them took the business very seriously, and they spent much of their time playing cards. Zosia loved to join the big boys because the store would always be full of laughter when they were working. They loved to tease and pinch their cute little cousin until her cheeks were burning, shouting "Zosia, Zosia, Zosia!" and tossing her from one to the other.

Within the happiness of Zosia's childhood, there had already been challenges and adjustments. Zosia had been three years old when Estera had taken her by the hand and introduced her to a very short, plain-looking woman.

"Zosia," Estera had said, "Panna Pola will be looking after you now."

Panna Pola — or Miss Pola — seemed kind enough, but Zosia had been confused. Wasn't her mother looking after her?

Since then, Zosia had never been allowed to play out of Panna Pola's sight, but she had quickly grown to love her caregiver. Before Zosia was old enough to go to school, Panna Pola took her every morning to Saski Park, where she ran along the winding paths through the trees and joined the other children at play.

Now that Zosia was a schoolgirl, Symcha escorted her to school in the morning. He walked her through their big gate, onto the bustling street where students rushed in and out of bookstores, and past the horse-drawn carriages called *dorozki* that waited for fares in front of the apartment block. Because it was December, the drivers flailed their arms and stamped their feet to keep warm. Sometimes, when Zosia was really lucky, the *dorozka* owned by Bracia Hoffenberg was waiting to drive her to her classes!

In the winter of her seventh year, little sister Zosia wanted to be just like her eldest sister Ruta, whose greenish eyes looked so dramatic set against her dark, wavy hair, and who studied fine arts at university. Sometimes Zosia sat beside Ruta as she painted bright, intricate images on fabrics and wooden objects. "Here, you try," Ruta said one evening. Ruta handed Zosia a piece of paper and she tried to copy a rose her sister had painted. When Ruta praised her, Zosia felt as if she were bursting with pride.

While they painted, Regina practised piano in the salon, serenading them with Mozart. Gina was an excellent pianist, but Zosia had little interest in music, so when Gina came to collect her for her lesson, she jumped out of her chair, ran to the elevator and went downstairs to play with her cousin.

Dark, handsome, and the only son, Heniek was the most spoiled of all the children. He was not an enthusiastic student but he was an excellent athlete — something his father didn't always appreciate. When Heniek arrived home from boxing practice with a bleeding nose, Symcha would ask, "Can't you find something more respectable to occupy your time?" Symcha would have preferred his son to be a scholar.

Every holiday, the entire Hoffenberg clan gathered in the fourteen-room apartment that Dziadek Gershon kept in the building that housed Bracia Hoffenberg. To Zosia, her father's father always seemed dissatisfied. He was stingy, too, despite his wealth, and rarely paid her any attention. Even when he did, she would shy away.

On Chanukah, the Jewish Festival of Lights, it was traditional to give gifts of money called Chanukah *gelt* to the children. But Gershon made no such provision. This Chanukah, as always, one of Zosia's uncles spun her around her grandfather until her head buzzed, and then another uncle, standing very close beside her grandfather, slipped five zlotys into her hand. As Zosia showed everyone her money, all her uncles smiled and nodded appreciatively at Gershon, but Zosia was not fooled.

Every Sunday afternoon, Estera's brother came to visit Zosia's family with his French wife. They had no children and they adored Zosia. Her uncle always brought her little presents. He would say, "Zosia, come, come!" and the two of them would go off in a corner and play cards.

Life was so easy for Zosia that it broke her heart to see her aunt and uncle working outside during the bitter Polish winter, selling coal from a shack that Symcha had built in the courtyard of one of the family businesses. Even in the shack, they froze because it was not heated. Symcha grumbled that they made so little money that he had to support them over the summer.

When winter passed and the warm months finally arrived, Zosia's parents left for the spa town of Marienbad in Czechoslovakia to holiday with friends, as they did every year — although sometimes they chose Karlsbad. They never took the children. Instead, Zosia and her siblings went with Panna Pola to Swider, one of the Polish resort areas popular with Jewish families.

In Swider, the Hoffenberg children, Panna Pola and a maid stayed in one half of a duplex. This year, the other half was occupied by the Bluman family. The Blumans also had four children: Lolek, Hela, Zygmunt and Natek.

When they returned from Marienbad, Symcha and Estera visited their offspring on weekends and brought them all sorts of treats: watermelons, candies and Zosia's favourite cakes.

Those summer days when her parents visited were the happiest times for six-year-old Zosia. Not only did she have her whole family with her, she received all sorts of attention from the older children next door. The boys gave her piggyback rides. She particularly liked Lolek who, at twenty-five, was the oldest son. Lolek was six foot four and, perched on his big, broad shoulders, she loved to tower over everyone.

There was one son Zosia didn't like: the youngest boy, Natek. He was the closest to her in age but, because he resented all the attention Zosia received, he taunted her and pulled her pigtails. She quickly learned to stay out of Natek's way.

2

The Shadows

I grew up in Burnaby, a largely working-class suburb of Vancouver, and in the long summer evenings, packs of us kids played kick the can for hours. When the sun set, the air rang with our mothers' voices as they shouted for us to come home. One by one, we would obey, but the next morning we would all regroup on the baseball diamond.

Despite the camaraderie, I always sensed that I was different from the other children in my neighbourhood. My brothers were the only other Jewish students at my school.

I recall that I didn't want to talk about the war. During slumber parties, when my friends shared stories about their fathers' wartime heroism, I would fall uncharacteristically silent. Even though my father had enlisted in the Canadian Army after his arrival in this country in 1941, to me he was not a war hero. And the war was not a time of glory; it was a time of suffering that set me apart.

I wanted my family to be more ordinary. I envied my friends whose fathers had normal jobs as firefighters, plumbers, longshoremen and carpenters. These men also did interesting things like fishing, hunting and camping with their families. None of them had funny accents. My father worked in a laboratory, which smelled terrible, and it was impossible to explain to my friends what he did. On the weekends, he liked to listen to classical music, including opera, and he had no idea how to hunt. His Polish accent embarrassed me almost as much as his European habit of kissing women's hands.

For my children — Michael, Danielle and Sam — it's completely different. They have never been able to get enough of talking about the war. In elementary school, all three of them were given an assignment to write about a hero. All three of them chose their grandmother. After my father passed away and my kids were teenagers, they spent hours with her, asking about her life in Warsaw and what happened when she and their grandfather tried to get out.

As I watched my children eagerly asking about their grandparents' lives during the war, I found their pride in their heritage to be infectious. For their sake, I resolved to record my mother's story, to write it all down in a book. Mom looked radiant as I interviewed her, especially when she talked about her father. But then my work as an arbitrator began to demand all my attention, and I promised myself that I would get back to my mother when I had more time.

Then a more serious distraction arrived. In the spring of 1999, my hand brushed down my breast and I felt a pebble about the size of a pea. The biopsy revealed cancer. I purchased a wig and sought out beautiful hats. I maintained my rigorous exercise regime and continued to work while under treatment. But I had little time to write.

Seven months later, my curls were back, softer than ever, and I felt energetic as I worked out on the Stairmaster at the gym. I pulled out my earlier writing and set to it again, but before long my breathing became strained and I needed more and more sleep. There were further tests, and then grim-faced doctors told me that I had colorectal cancer. It had already begun to spread.

This time I did not stop writing. I stopped working instead. The treatment, which I am in the midst of as I complete this manuscript, is time-consuming, and intensely unpleasant. I devote the little time I have left each day to telling my mother's story.

With each new health crisis, my motivation for writing is becoming more complex. At first, I simply wanted to ensure that my mother's legacy would pass to my three children. Then I wanted to connect to my parents' generation and breathe meaning back into the few tangible objects — the letters, the photographs — that they still had. But now my mother's story has become my story. With each tinge of nausea, each cramp in my belly, I say to myself, "Don't you want to know what lurks in the shadows, waiting to be revealed?" ≋

3

Chocolates and Ice Cream

GROWING UP, ZOSIA learned that she belonged in Warsaw. She
also learned that romance tastes like chocolate.

Poland was a poor country and the Hoffenberg family's maids,
especially the Jewish ones, comforted themselves, as they lay down
on their hard cots in the kitchen, with dreams of going to America.
But going to America was not an aspiration for Zosia's family, for
Symcha was deeply committed to Poland. Life there was good to
him and his family.

Warsaw was a cultured and energetic metropolis with a Jewish
population of 350,000, close to one-third of the city's total. Jewish
intellectuals were prominent within Polish society; Julian Tuwim
and Antoni Slonimski, both Jews, were the best-loved poets in a
country that loved poetry. There was Jewish theatre and there were

many Jewish newspapers. Jews and Gentiles alike would turn on their radios to hear the child-rearing advice of Janusz Korczak, a respected and beloved Jewish pediatrician, the Polish Dr. Spock.

True, Jews were discriminated against in university admissions, but many went abroad to study, and came back to Warsaw as doctors and lawyers. Symcha felt that anti-Semitism in Poland was to be expected; no European or North American country was free of such prejudice, and Polish Jews were fortunate in that they had not been victims of terrible pogroms or restricted in where they could live, as they had been in Tsarist Russia.

The wall safe in Symcha's study was hidden behind a large portrait of Napoleon, who was widely admired for commanding a Polish regiment that had supposedly been free of prejudice.

"We are fortunate to live in Poland," Symcha told Zosia. "We do not have to hide our identity, and we are free to practise our religion." And, as he often pointed out, he had a flourishing business with the Polish government. Even as war with Germany became imminent, Symcha scoffed at the suggestion of leaving his home. "Why would I leave Warsaw?" he asked. "It's the new Jerusalem!"

Some citizens of the new Jerusalem still followed traditional ways. The popularity of marriage through a matchmaker was in decline by the late 1920s and early 1930s, but the custom still dictated the unions of Zosia's sisters Ruta and Gina. Beautiful, artistic, twenty-two-year-old Ruta was a prize, so it was not surprising when her cousin Pavel fell in love with her.

Symcha opposed marriage between relatives and he tried to reason with Pavel. "Look at poor Hinda!" he said, referring to his sister and her mentally handicapped child. But Pavel insisted that he was in love with Ruta, and would continue to pursue her.

Symcha summoned a matchmaker, who provided them with a long list of eligible suitors. "Just meet some of them," Symcha urged his daughter. Declaring her love for Pavel, Ruta refused, but after shedding many tears, she finally relented and agreed to meet another young man. Pavel, who lived with his parents in the same building as the Hoffenberg family, saw her with the new suitor and started screaming. Ruta was ordered not to speak to Pavel again and, as far as Zosia knew, she abided by her father's command.

But Ruta was fussy, and no one lived up to her Pavel — until she was introduced to Julek Fishbajn. He was tall, with dark hair, deep brown eyes and strong, even features. He came from a wealthy, highly respectable family and had a successful business of his own supplying flour to bakeries. After their first meeting, Ruta agreed to let Julek see her again. Symcha and Estera were delighted and, over the next few months, Julek made regular visits to the Hoffenbergs' apartment.

Each time before he arrived, the furniture in the salon was stripped of its protective white covers, revealing the highly polished mahogany with its elaborate gold trim. The maids hummed good-naturedly as they worked, since they could always expect a hefty tip from Julek. Zosia also revelled in his visits because he brought silk-covered boxes filled with the finest chocolates in Warsaw. She was not allowed to join the young couple in the salon but, first thing the next morning, nine-year-old Zosia ran in and gorged on the sweets.

After several months' courtship the young couple decided to marry, and, when the Hoffenbergs agreed to provide a dowry of 10,000 American dollars, the bargain was sealed.

Julek gave Ruta a giant diamond engagement ring and continued to shower her with jewels after they were married. Still, Zosia could tell that Ruta had little in common with Julek, and they were not really friends. It saddened her to see that her talented, well-educated sister was bored and intellectually under-challenged.

Gina was also married through a matchmaker. Jurek Goldkorn

owned a factory that produced crystal ware from raw glass imported from Czechoslovakia. Julek and Jurek's names were almost identical, but Jurek made a less impressive suitor. He was big enough, but not really tall. He was sufficiently well-to-do, but neither as wealthy — nor as generous to Zosia — as Ruta's Julek. Perhaps most importantly to Zosia, the chocolates that he had brought during the courtship were not nearly as good.

When she became a teenager, Zosia loved romance. She borrowed library books that featured wicked stepmothers, terrible schoolmistresses or heroines who threw themselves into their lovers' arms — anything that would make her sob. Her sisters' cool, business-like marriages paled in comparison to her ideas of passion. When Symcha teased her, saying, "For you, I will pick a husband with a big hump on his back!" Zosia retorted, "I will pick my own husband!" And she reminded her father of her intention time and again.

Rakish Heniek shared his youngest sister's view of the matter. He had had many girlfriends and absolutely refused to consider an arranged marriage. His father appeared adamant, but Heniek declined to meet any of the girls recommended by the matchmakers. He had already settled on Olga, whom he wanted to marry. She had blond hair with a slight reddish tint, very blue eyes, high cheekbones and a warm smile. Symcha and Estera did not approve of Olga for many reasons — not the least of which was that she came from a family of assimilated Jews — but finally, after months of arguing, Symcha and Estera relented and accepted Olga as their son's fiancée.

By the summer of 1938, war was on everyone's minds, but Zosia was seventeen and enjoying her life. She went with Ruta and her daughter Hanusia to the resort at Druskieniki, where she had her own room in the villa.

Boys sometimes paid her attention, and one sweet, red-haired young lad was particularly persistent, but none of these flirtations went very far. Then, one hot day, Zosia was eating a scoop of ice cream that she'd just bought from a vendor when a giant of a man approached her, grandly bowed, and kissed her hand. "Beautiful Zosia!" he said.

It was Lolek Bluman, who had given her so many piggyback rides when he had lived next door in Swider. Since then, she had run into him occasionally in the cafés in Warsaw, and he had always made a strong impression. He was rich and handsome, towered over most of the population, and had an intriguing reputation as a shameless playboy: he lived openly with a Gentile woman and it was said that he had the most lavish and raucous parties with dozens more women on hand. He was twenty years older than Zosia but, like most women, she could not help being charmed by his courtly manners.

He seemed to like Zosia too, because he called his younger brother Natek up to the ice cream vendor's kiosk and introduced him to her.

"I think I know you," she said shyly.

Natek looked perplexed.

"One summer — I think I was six years old — my family shared the cabin next to yours in Swider," she explained. She did not add that he'd been a nasty boy who had pulled her pigtails.

"Natek and I have been in Grodno on business," explained Lolek, "buying cucumbers for pickles. We're here to have fun for two days before we go back to Warsaw. May we come visit you later?"

"Of course," Zosia replied, trying to conceal her excitement.

That afternoon the two brothers came to her room. As they talked, it struck Zosia that Natek, who seemed very nice, was becoming more animated. When they left, however, neither brother said anything about seeing her again, and Zosia was disappointed. But the next morning, to her surprise, Natek arrived at her door. "Would you like to come for a walk?" he asked quietly.

It was exciting to walk alongside a twenty-four-year-old university graduate! And, because Natek was 5'11", Zosia finally did not feel embarrassed at being so tall; at 5'7", she was the same height as her father and had always been the tallest in her class. He took her back to her room and promised to return to Druskieniki to see her again.

He did come back later that summer and, when Zosia returned to Warsaw, they met at a popular café. And this time, Natek made no attempt to hide his feelings for her: he wanted to see her every day.

Zosia was thrilled, but nervous, too. She felt certain that her parents would never approve. For a few weeks, she met Natek surreptitiously, but she lived in terror of getting caught and couldn't bear the thought of how betrayed her father would feel. Finally, she summoned the courage to tell her parents. As she'd expected, they were opposed to her stepping out with any boy, much less — as Symcha pointed out — the brother of a notorious playboy.

"Why do you blame him because of his brother?" Zosia shot back. "Natek is different."

The room was silent as Symcha considered his daughter's determined face. He knew that Zosia would never agree to an arranged marriage. Finally, he acknowledged that, except for the eldest son, the Bluman family was highly conservative, and that in many respects Natek was a suitable match. He gave Zosia permission to continue seeing her suitor. He wasn't disappointed, though, when he discovered that Natek would soon be leaving the country.

I first saw Drew Schroeder in the summer of 1973 when I was working at the law library at the University of British Columbia doing research for one of my professors. When Drew walked in with his full beard and long hair, he looked as though he had stepped right out of the movie version of *Jesus Christ, Superstar*.

He must have sensed a kindred spirit beneath my black Afro and granny glasses because we were soon chatting. Drew confessed that he was in the library because he was terrified. A Rhodes Scholar, he had done his law degree at Oxford and, upon graduation, he had immediately been headhunted to teach at UBC. He was about to step in front of second-year classes and he was afraid that his students would know more about Canadian law than he did. I don't know if he felt better or worse when he found out that I was going to be one of those students. Drew was scheduled to teach a course in real estate law that I had registered for.

We went for coffee and instantly discovered a common interest in left-wing politics. Protests against the war in Vietnam were in full swing, and I had participated in a sit-in at the university's Faculty Club. I think I impressed Drew when I told him it was the best party I'd ever been to.

Drew was married at the time but, when he and his wife separated the next summer, we could finally date — officially.

Five years later, when I phoned my folks to tell them that Drew and I were getting married, my father was so furious that I was going to wed a Gentile that he slammed the phone down. My mother told me that he shouted, "If they marry, they won't be allowed in this house!" But she replied, "You are going to accept who your daughter is marrying and they are going to be in our house. That's the end of it." ⌇

Natek had wanted to study architecture, but when his father Szaja insisted that he take a degree that related to the Bluman family

27

business, Natek had reluctantly complied. Szaja Bluman's company, Kaefka, imported dried fruits and nuts. It also processed pickles, candies, jams and canned fruits in its factory, largely for export to the United States. Now, Zosia learned, Szaja wanted his son to learn American distribution methods, so Natek would be going to New York to spend a year working for his father's associate Mr. Catz, who was part-owner of a large American company. By the time Natek met Zosia, it was too late to change the arrangements. But he was deeply in love and pleaded with her to come with him.

"That's impossible," she told him. "My father would never agree."

Natek was reluctant to leave but he really had no choice, and he could not deny that, given the state of Europe in the fall of 1938, it would be prudent to establish connections in America. Zosia would have preferred to go on gossiping with her girlfriends rather than talk about politics, but it was becoming impossible to ignore the rising tensions in Europe. Polish Jews who had been expelled from Germany after living there for decades told her how they had lost their jobs and then their assets before being thrown out of the country. Still, life carried on normally in Warsaw. The cafés were full and everyone was dancing; Zosia took comfort in that. Reports from the countryside of riots and anti-Semitic attacks were nothing new. Some of her friends had seen fascist youth marching in the streets of Warsaw, waving their fists and shouting anti-Semitic slogans, but even these friends refused to become alarmed. "These things happen in cycles," they said. "In time, such things will pass. Besides, Poland needs us. And it would be impossible to get rid of so many people. Where could they send us?"

Still, every time she turned on the radio, Zosia heard the harsh voice of Adolph Hitler threatening her country; his troops had solidified their control of Austria and the Sudetenland and now he was making claims to parts of Poland.

With so much else on her mind, the day of Natek's departure came surprisingly quickly for Zosia. As he said goodbye and boarded the train that would take him to his ship, she tried unsuccessfully to hide her tears. She had learned from the movies that American girls were all smart and glamorous. As she watched the train chug away, she was convinced that Natek would fall in love with one of those girls and forget all about her.

For a while, she heard nothing from him, and became despondent. Then a long, wonderful letter arrived and, from then on, there was a letter it seemed almost every day. Natek gave her detailed impressions of America. He attended the New York World's Fair and was fascinated by it, particularly the complicated push-button light display at the General Electric pavilion. And, in one letter after another, he professed his love for her. He wrote as if their marriage were inevitable and, though a year was a long time to wait, Zosia could not imagine being with anyone but him.

In New York, Natek lived in a small apartment on Lexington Avenue and saved his wages. He wrote to Zosia that he was placing the money in an American bank account so that they would have access to it if they ever went abroad, either by choice or by necessity. From American newspapers, he learned that the situation in Europe was even more alarming than he had realized, and he warned Zosia that all Jews would be wise to leave Europe for America. Even in New York, he saw Aryans parading down the streets, waving flags, touting their victories and proclaiming their superiority. And the situation of Jews in Germany was far worse than the Polish press had made evident. "Your family must make arrangements to leave," he urged. "Soon it will be too late."

He pleaded with Zosia to come, even if her family would not; the two of them could be married as soon as she arrived. She was afraid to ask her parents, though, and simply wrote that they would never agree.

By mid-1939, Natek was desperate. He was convinced that war might begin any day and could not bear the thought that he might be forever separated from Zosia. His visa did not expire until November and he wanted to stay in the United States — in fact Mr. Catz had offered to sponsor him, Zosia and his whole family as immigrants — but Zosia wrote in letter after letter that her parents would not let her come. And Natek could not stay in New York without her. He realized that no amount of pleading on Zosia's part would change her parents' minds; he would have to go back to Warsaw and convince them. So, in July of 1939, he started for home.

4

Fire

ZOSIA WAS OVERJOYED when Natek returned to Warsaw, but she still insisted that she could not leave for America without her parents' permission. She was too young!

"Don't you realize how little time we have left?" he asked. "You've read my letters. Poland is next on Hitler's list!"

"I would miss my family too much," she said.

Natek went to see Symcha.

"Pan Hoffenberg," he began, respectfully addressing Symcha with the formal "Pan," "what you've got here will not be worth anything once the war comes. In New York, they're saying that things look very bad in Europe — for Jews in particular."

Symcha had just returned from a business trip to Bulgaria.

"What do you know?" he asked his daughter's young suitor.

"I've been abroad and zlotys are as good as gold. So Germans come. I was here when they came during the First World War and the Germans were gentlemen. If it were Russians, then I'd be worried!"

But events soon made Natek's pleas academic. At three o'clock in the morning on the first of September — Zosia's nineteenth birthday — the Hoffenbergs were awakened by screaming sirens. They ran to the cellar with the other tenants as they'd all been instructed to do. The sirens had gone off before, for practice drills, and Zosia assumed that this was just another false alarm but, within minutes, they heard airplanes overhead and the thudding of bombs. The Germans. It was hot and crowded in the cellar and, when a baby began to wail, the people were so worried that they verbally abused its mother.

Eventually the baby stopped crying and everyone became quiet. Then, after a very long hour, the all-clear siren sounded and everyone rushed up to the street, only to find the air filled with dust. Thinking it might be gas, people panicked, and they shoved children and old women out of the way as they scrambled to return to their homes.

Before the air raid, Jurek had told Zosia he would give her a gold bracelet for her birthday if Gina gave birth to a boy. Although Gina had had a son, Zosia never received her bracelet. In fact, her birthday was not celebrated at all.

From the moment the siren woke her, Zosia's life was transformed. The Germans bombed the power plant on the first day, cutting off the electricity and, within days, the telephone and water were out as well. The maids left the apartment. The bombing could come at any time but it usually happened at night or in the early morning. It was impossible for Zosia to get a proper sleep because she was constantly running down to the crowded cellar. Even

Zosia Hoffenberg as a young woman at age nineteen

Natek Bluman, c. 1939–40

Lolek's wife Danka. A *Volksdeutsche*, Danka was able to
travel relatively easily within Nazi-occupied Poland.

Natek's brother Lolek Bluman, c. 1955

Saski Park, Warsaw, in happier days before the German
aerial bombardment of September 1939

The gateway to the public market in Warsaw,
which was reduced to rubble as a result of the
German aerial attack, September 1939.

Two boys pull a sled through the streets of Warsaw
after the German bombing, 1939.

Women and children rescuing items from a
bombed-out house in Warsaw, 1939.
PHOTO CREDIT: *United States Holocaust Memorial Museum*

worse than the bombs were the artillery shells fired from the German guns that surrounded the city. Zosia could at least hear the planes before the bombs fell, but the guns could start firing at any time and it was impossible to predict which direction the shells would come from. Every time she left the apartment, her life was at risk.

After four days of bombing, rumours circulated that the Germans were on the verge of entering Warsaw, and orders were issued over giant megaphones for all young men to evacuate the city so that they could avoid capture and defend eastern Poland. Zosia's brother Heniek prepared to leave, and Natek came to tell her that he was going east with his father and his brothers Lolek and Zygmunt, as well as Danka, Lolek's Gentile girlfriend.

Danka was a *Volksdeutsche*, a Pole of German heritage from the region of Poland that had been annexed from Germany after World War I. The Nazis had conferred citizenship on all *Volksdeutsche*, so Danka had German papers. Zosia had met her a few times and had observed on each occasion how Danka adored Lolek. "He is fortunate to have her," Natek had said. "He's always running around with other women, and I'm not sure why she stays. Danka is very capable." Danka's relationship with Lolek had been a scandal up to that point, but none of the Bluman men complained as she and her German documents joined them for the trip east.

Natek had a plan. "With a few others, I will go to Romania and contact Mr. Catz to see what he can do to get us into the United States," he explained to Zosia, referring to his friend and business associate in America. "I will come back for you and your family when we have the papers arranged."

With the young men — including Zosia's brother and suitor — leaving, Warsaw became a city populated only by women, children and old people.

Then, terrible news: Ruta, Zosia's dearest sister, was in the hospital, badly wounded. She had been in the local library when a shell ripped through the roof. The family rushed to be with her. "My poor Ruta," Julek moaned. "What if she dies? And what if the diamonds are gone?" He had invested in a diamond necklace for Ruta as a precaution in case the war made his zlotys worthless.

But Ruta was still alive, and she still had the jewels with her. She had suffered a head injury, however, and she could not speak. Zosia was chilled when she saw her sister's beautiful green eyes looking around blankly and her sister's mouth silenced.

Polish hospitals were unreliable — people who could afford it preferred to be treated at home whenever possible — and the meagre resources of this one were further strained as newly injured patients arrived every minute. Julek went to the administrator and offered the hospital all the flour it could possibly require. Ruta received excellent care.

With his father and brothers, Natek joined thousands of people streaming out of the city. The Blumans had the luxury of an automobile, while most were on foot. They eventually ran out of gas, however, and had to join the refugees who were walking, hitchhiking, and jumping onto passing trains — whatever would get them out of Poland.

When the Blumans finally reached the border, they faced a wall of less-than-welcoming Romanian soldiers — Romania was officially neutral but was clearly unwilling to accept a flood of foreigners — so they retreated to the Polish town of Czestkow to figure out a way to get across.

The Bluman men had still not come up with a plan on September 17, when the Soviet Union entered the war and invaded eastern Poland. The Blumans were now in Soviet territory. Deciding that it was hopeless to try to get out, and that they would be better off in a larger city, Natek and his family made their way to Lvov.

In the Hoffenbergs' apartment in Warsaw, people were sleeping on the floor, eating whatever they could, and constantly nagging each other. Estera's parents had moved away to the country in 1938 but had moved back when the war started. Gina, Jurek and their baby boy Grzesio moved in too. After the second week of bombing, everyone moved to Gina's apartment a few blocks away; it was smaller, but located on the first floor and less vulnerable to damage from the bombs. Wanting to be ready for the war, Symcha had stockpiled American money. That cash — and the silverware — changed apartments along with the family.

When Heniek went east, he left his wife Olga alone in their apartment and, several days into the blitzkrieg, she finally invited Zosia to move in with her. Even that relative spaciousness was short-lived, however. The other tenants decided that Olga's ground-floor suite was the safest in the building, so they all moved in.

Every day, soldiers returning from the front streamed through Warsaw on their way east, some on horseback, some on foot. Covered in blood and dirt, many with festering wounds, they had been no match for the German air cover and tanks. Hordes of scared, exhausted refugees followed behind them on foot. Zosia joined those who were handing out food and coffee to the ragged procession. A skinny young man tottered past, clutching a dirty pack. "Zosia," he said. It took a moment for her to recognize him: he was the red-haired boy she had flirted with at Druskieniki in the summer.

Almost a month passed, and the Polish government remained defiant. Then, on September 26, the Germans sent hundreds of planes over Warsaw and bombed the city relentlessly. Convinced the apartment would be hit, Zosia and Olga ran outside, where they were momentarily deafened by the din of falling bombs. They fled through the streets looking for a place to hide, but flames rose from almost every building. Each time a plane flew overhead, they hid in the nearest doorway. Then they saw a bomb pulverize the building directly across the street from them, and they took flight, shrieking. Zosia was convinced that she was about to die. She prayed that the government would finally surrender, because what could be worse than this?

After twenty-four hours of ceaseless bombing, Poland surrendered. The bombs stopped.

With the city in flames, Zosia summoned the courage to go back and check on her family. As she and Olga ran through the streets, all of Warsaw seemed to be on fire. Scorched bodies lay everywhere and the two women had to jump over them again and again. The heat was unbearable, and gusts of wind sent the flames into the middle of the street. Zosia's hair caught fire and she screamed hysterically but was not seriously hurt.

When they arrived at Gina's apartment, there was nothing but a smouldering heap. The building was gone. With hearts pounding, they ran to the Bracia Hoffenberg building and were relieved to find that apartment block intact. Zosia found her family inside. It was only after five minutes of kissing and hugging that she realized her mother was not there. Everyone had run in different directions when Gina's apartment block had been hit, and they'd lost Estera among the hordes. Gina's husband Jurek went out to look for her. Symcha had lost all of his valuables at Gina's — the silverware, the American dollars — and he paced back and forth, asking, "What shall become of us?"

After three days, Estera found her way back to the Hoffenbergs' apartment, having survived on the few candies she had in her purse. And, with the bombing halted, Ruta regained her speech. But no one felt like rejoicing. The streets were silent as everyone waited for the German soldiers to arrive.

Zosia stood at an apartment window that faced Marszalkowska Street, the thoroughfare that passed the Bracia Hoffenberg building, and watched the conquering army march past. Poles had been warned not to stand too close to the windows, but Zosia stayed in her spot for every last soldier and tank. The procession lasted a full day. Every so often, the soldiers would stop to eat and she would look on with envy as they pulled succulent-looking sausages out of their packs.

The Hoffenbergs were luckier than most because Ruta's husband Julek was able to supply them with all the flour they needed, but they still required other staples and had to line up at the stores. The queues were supervised by Germans in SS uniforms. As Zosia stood waiting, she saw a Pole signal to an SS officer, then point to a Jew and shout, "*Jude!*" The Jew was thrown out of the line. Zosia went weak in the knees and almost fainted. This happened time and again. Eventually, she came to expect it.

Zosia was lucky. If they spoke Polish at all, most Polish Jews had Yiddish accents that gave them away, even if their features did not fit the Jewish stereotype. But Zosia and her siblings grew up speaking Polish exclusively. With her blue eyes and impeccable speech, the SS would not immediately suspect that she was Jewish.

Before the war, Warsaw had bubbled with throngs of people. Now the bombed-out streets were silent. Many, especially Jews, had tried to escape to the east but, after the Soviet occupation, most had given up and returned home. The Germans began to post orders on the walls of buildings, first imposing rules such as curfews on the whole population, then specific measures that applied only to Jews. Rumours circulated that they were going to establish a Jewish ghetto.

Whenever Symcha went out, the family fretted that he might not come back because, with his long beard and Yiddish accent, he was an obvious target for the Germans. On one occasion he returned, white-faced and shaking, his clothes in tatters. Some soldiers had pushed him into a van, handed him a shovel and then ordered him out to clean the streets. He could not restrain his tears as he explained what had happened. A few days later, he came home with his clothes dishevelled, his face blotchy, and his eyes darting everywhere. Germans had stopped him on the sidewalk and pulled him around by his beard.

Estera was home alone when three soldiers came to search the apartment. They found the safe and insisted that Estera open it. When she told them she did not have the key, they slapped and pushed her. After that, Estera was so frightened that the family could not leave her by herself.

Terrified, Zosia seldom went out at this time, but even in the apartment she felt as if she were always waiting for a knock on the door. At night, she'd wake up whenever she heard a noise in the stairwell, and then she would wonder where Natek was, or if he were even alive.

One day in December, Zosia was surprised to see a petite blond woman at her door.

"Danka!" she exclaimed. It was Lolek's girlfriend. "When did you get back to Warsaw?"

"I've come from Lvov, to deliver this from Natek." Danka handed her a letter. "He and Heniek are both there."

Zosia barely had time to absorb the fact that Natek and her brother had somehow managed to find one another. Danka was explaining that she had offered to go back to Warsaw because it would be safer for her to cross from Soviet- to German-occupied territory than it would for a Jew.

"They were really glad I went east with them," she was saying, "because I have German papers, and I helped Lolek with the driving."

Zosia couldn't help remembering how the Blumans had felt about Danka before the war. And Symcha and Estera had been even more judgmental.

As soon as Danka left, Zosia carefully opened the letter. The instant she saw Natek's handwriting, she began to cry. How she longed for him at that moment! He assured her that they were all well, but he missed her terribly and Heniek missed Olga. They wanted the two of them to leave Warsaw immediately; Danka would accompany them over the border.

Zosia wanted to rush into Symcha's study to tell him the good news. But what could she say? She was nineteen years old and could not contemplate going without her papa's permission. A few months earlier, she had asked him if she could holiday abroad and he had told her that it was too dangerous. Besides, she still barely knew Natek; their deepest contact had been through lengthy letters. So how could she ask for her father's permission to go on a treacherous journey led by a Gentile woman with a bad reputation, to join the lines of refugees crossing the war-ravaged countryside? How could she ask permission to enter a territory controlled by the Russians, whom he despised? He would never agree to it.

Uncertain what to do, Zosia read the letter over and over again. She missed Natek and, if she did not go now, she might never see him again. Perhaps her assumptions about Symcha were wrong. Her father, who had once been so optimistic and extroverted, now paced the apartment looking confused and defeated. She had overheard him asking Estera, "How was I to know?" He was tormented by his complacency, his refusal even to consider taking his family out of Poland. "And if the business falls apart, what will become of us?"

Zosia decided that she had to ask for his permission.

She knocked on the door of Symcha's study. He was sitting at his polished mahogany desk. His clear blue eyes looked dim.

"I have good news," she said. "Danka was here with a letter from Natek. He says that Heniek is with him in Lvov, and everyone is fine."

Symcha sat up straight.

"Would you like to read it, Tatus?" she asked.

Symcha put his glasses on and read the letter. She sat and watched him. Finally, he put the paper down and stared at her.

"I really want to see Natek," she said. "May I go with Danka and Olga?"

"You're too young to leave home."

"Please, Tatus, please. Olga will be with me. I know we'll be safe."

He looked so sad and distracted that he reminded her of a picture she'd seen of the ancient Jews, exiled from Jerusalem. She felt terrible telling him that she wanted to leave his side.

"Please, Tatus. If I don't go, I may never see Natek again. Staying here is just as dangerous!"

"But you are just a child. You need your family."

"I am not a child. And I won't be gone forever."

He looked away.

"If you really want to go — go," he said softly. "But only for two weeks."

"Okay. Two weeks."

She would have agreed to anything.

Symcha rose and walked over to the wall. He removed the painting of Napoleon, opened his safe and took out 150 zlotys and two crisp American two-dollar bills.

"Your zlotys will be worthless once you cross the border." He placed the money in the folds of a leather belt, and handed it to her. "It will be safe hidden here."

≋. When my mother opened her front door and saw my boyfriend Drew for the first time, she startled and stepped back. She looked so shocked that I asked, "What's the matter?"

She paused for a moment before replying, "I don't believe it. He's the image of my father." ≋

5

A Shared Sofa Bed

DANKA HAD TOLD ZOSIA that, because the train could not cross the border between the Soviet and German sectors of Poland, they would have to travel on foot sometimes. So Zosia packed only the barest essentials in her knapsack. Aside from the ski boots, the ski pants and the warm fur coat she wore to protect herself from the frigid Polish winter, Zosia took only two dresses, a change of underwear, a nightgown, a toothbrush and a comb. Because she was planning to return in two weeks, she did not pack any photographs of her family.

She met Olga and Danka at the station. They said little as they waited. Finally, a dingy freight train pulled up to the platform. They climbed into a rusty cattle car, cleared a space on the dirty floor and sat. Immediately, Zosia was struck by a deep sadness. She hadn't realized how much she would miss her family. Remembering how desolate Symcha had looked when he gave her permission to go, she started to cry. For a moment she even considered jumping out of the rail car while the train was still idling.

She couldn't help wondering if she was making a terrible decision. Could Natek really be as wonderful as his letters had been? She had hardly seen him for a year. And who were these two women she was travelling with? She was suddenly convinced that she would never see Tatus or the rest of her family again.

Then her rational mind told her that it was natural to fear the unknown. She loved Natek, didn't she? She was going to him. The train started to roll.

Five kilometres from the border, Zosia, Danka and Olga disembarked. They were not sure which direction to start walking, and they summoned the courage to ask an Austrian soldier for help. Olga and Zosia remained quiet as Danka showed the soldier her German papers and explained that she and her friends lived in the Russian-occupied area of Poland, that they needed to know where the border was so that they could return to their families. The soldier pointed the way. He seemed very pleasant.

It was extremely cold as they trudged over the countryside. Fortunately, Zosia's coat was lined with otter fur and she reminded herself how lucky she was to have it. They met many other refugees as they walked, and everyone gave them advice.

"It's a game of wits, crossing the border."

"If you get caught, never tell them where you really want to go."

"Yes, if you want to go to Warsaw, tell them you are going to the Russian zone and you will be certain to be sent to Warsaw."

"And it's exactly the same the other way round."

A few hours later, the three women came face-to-face with a party of Russian soldiers. They wore their winter uniforms, including pointed hats with flaps on either side to cover their ears, and at first Zosia had to tighten her lips to suppress a giggle. But she wasn't laughing when she and the others were thrown to the ground, and the soldiers ran their hands up and down them, feeling for weapons. Zosia found her body growing stiff, as if she were no longer in it, and when the women were ordered to their feet, she had trouble standing. Then the soldiers led them to a small building and shut them in a room along with fifty other people squeezed together.

No one could go to the bathroom without a soldier accompanying them. Eventually, Zosia could wait no longer and asked to go. As she lowered her underpants, the soldier's eyes stayed on her. Her bladder was full, but it took several moments before she could relax enough to relieve herself.

After two days in these conditions, Zosia, Olga, and Danka were taken to see the border patrol officer. An expressionless Russian soldier, he asked where they were going. Again, Danka spoke for them.

"We want to go back to our families in Warsaw."

"*Nyet!*" he barked.

When he ordered them to go to the Russian zone, they tried to look disappointed.

Trudging towards Lvov, they became more and more hungry, and their knapsacks seemed to grow heavier and heavier as the hours passed. A man who seemed friendly offered to carry Olga's backpack. She handed it to him, and an instant later he had disappeared, along with all of her belongings. Zosia and Danka tried to console her, but Olga was furious with herself for being so naïve.

Just when they could not bear walking any farther in the bitter cold, they came to a little station where a train was about to leave for Lvov, and they climbed aboard. When they arrived in the city, they clambered off and Danka led them through the streets towards Lolek and Natek's apartment.

"But where can I find Heniek?" asked Olga.

Danka directed her and, just before Olga set off to reunite with her husband, Zosia felt so sorry for her sister-in-law that she gave her a dress and her one extra pair of underwear.

Suddenly, she recognized Natek walking along the street! She shouted and waved until he saw her. Then Natek ran towards her, grabbed her and kissed her again and again. He couldn't stop saying, "You made it! You made it!"

Clearly, Zosia's arrival was a great relief to Natek. But, even as she walked along with him and Danka, Zosia could feel the return of the loneliness that had ambushed her when she boarded the train. She was happy to see him, but not as happy as she had hoped. She missed her parents and sisters and doubted whether Natek could fill that void.

The atmosphere in Lvov was less repressive than in Warsaw. She did not find the Soviets nearly as intimidating as the Nazis and, if she ignored them, they ignored her. There were no regulations directed specifically against Jews. And, thankfully, money was not a problem. Zosia had been able to exchange one of the two-dollar bills for 850 rubles, and a good meal only cost two. Still, Zosia could not shake off her uncertainty and the depression that came with it.

Natek wanted to get married immediately, but who was he, really? Accepting his proposal would change her life completely. Coming to meet him in Lvov had been romantic, but also more real and frightening than their excited exchange of letters. Could she really imagine lying next to him every night? Raising children together? One day, as Natek was laying out plans for their future, she allowed herself to study his face. What she saw was a serious, diligent man who loved her passionately. With a feeling that flooded through her body like a deep blush, she realized that, now that she was in Lvov, marriage to Natek was inevitable. It had not been so obvious when she stood in her father's study pleading for permission to go and see him. But the war had thrust her into adulthood, and she sensed that her fate was inextricably tied to Natek Bluman's.

≋ When Drew and his wife separated, one of the first things we did with our newfound freedom was to go camping.

After a day on the highway, I was becoming a bit grumpy as we drove forty miles up a bumpy logging road along the White River in the interior of British Columbia. It was about nine at night before we inflated our air mattresses and pitched our pup tent near the water.

When the sun woke me up the next morning, I slipped out of the tent quietly so that I wouldn't waken Drew. The morning light on the mountains took my breath away, and the air felt so glorious on my naked skin that I decided to bathe in the river.

I had almost finished when Drew bolted out of the tent and came stumbling towards me. "For Christ's sake," he shouted. "This is an active logging road! In the summertime, those guys start at, like, four in the morning. There are going to be trucks past here any minute and if one of those loggers sees you like that, we're going to have about twenty of them here in no time, and there's going to be a real problem!"

He was so beside himself that I couldn't resist teasing him a bit. I didn't say a word, but I climbed out of the river, my skin singing from the icy water. I stretched my best feline stretch and, as I walked silently past Drew, I gave him a look that let him know that I didn't think twenty loggers sounded like such a bad idea! ≋

Zosia most certainly loved Natek. And she desired him, too. Natek had rented a single room in an apartment where the two of them shared a too-short sofa bed. Respecting the strict Orthodox code, Zosia resisted having sex with him until they were married but, as her depression lifted, she realized that she was as impatient as he was to have the wedding.

The first test of her resolve came quickly. About ten days after Zosia's arrival in Lvov, a friend from Warsaw arrived with a message from Symcha.

"Your father is well," Sabina Zimmerman said, "but he misses you. He asked me to tell you to come back to Warsaw immediately. He also said that you are not to get married in Lvov. You must come back to Warsaw if you and Natek decide to marry. He wants to be at your wedding."

In the days that followed, Zosia agonized over her father's message. Symcha had provided love and security her entire life, but large numbers of Jewish refugees were coming into Lvov with reports of refugees disappearing on their way to Lvov or on their way back to Warsaw. Tension between the Germans and Soviets had been increasing, which made approaching the border even riskier.

"We must get married here," Natek said. "Your father should realize that what he wants is not possible."

Zosia had never disobeyed her father, but this was an unprecedented situation. It was impossible to predict when it would be safe to return to Warsaw. Sabina was going to marry her boyfriend, and she wanted them all to get married together in Lvov. Zosia finally said yes. A rabbi was consulted and, on December 26, 1939, in a double ceremony, the two couples were wed in a synagogue. Zosia's dear Tatus was not there, but Natek's father Szaja and brother Zygmunt, as well as Danka, Lolek and Heniek, all celebrated with the young newlyweds.

After the wedding, Natek seemed determined to prove himself a capable protector. He spent every hour plotting how to get out of

Lvov. Everyone understood that the truce between Germany and the Soviet Union was fragile. Natek was sure that it was just a matter of time before the Germans invaded. It was crucial that they get out of the country for other reasons, too. Every person arriving in Lvov was required to register with the authorities and to state his occupation in order to obtain the necessary permit to stay. The Soviets had been impressed with Natek's credentials as an agricultural engineer and had offered him a job deep inside Russia. Natek had no desire to go and he worried that, before long, he would not have a choice.

Natek's plan was to return to the United States — for the duration of the war only. That would require finding an American consulate from which he could cable Mr. Catz in order to ask for his assistance in obtaining a visa.

Natek decided that they ought to go to Lithuania, for there were consulates operating in Kaunas, the capital, from which he could cable Mr. Catz. And, while they were in Lithuania, they could stay in Vilnius, where there was a large Polish-speaking population. The only catch to Natek's plan was that leaving Lvov would require exit visas, and they had been told that requesting one could result in deportation to Siberia.

"We will have to steal across the border," Natek said.

Zosia was confident that her intelligent and resourceful new husband knew what he was doing, and she agreed. Lolek was just as eager to go to America, so he and Danka decided to cross to Lithuania too. But no matter how earnestly Natek tried to persuade them, Olga and Heniek were not prepared to leave Europe.

"If I had my jewels," Olga said, "then maybe."

"What could I do in the United States?" asked Heniek. He told Zosia that he could not run from his responsibilities in the family business. Leaving Poland for a country he knew little about, where his prospects would be so uncertain, was inconceivable. Natek's father Szaja and his brother Zygmunt shared Heniek's reservations. Sabina wanted to join them but her husband refused.

In the middle of January 1940, they all parted ways. Natek, Zosia, Lolek, and Danka headed towards Lithuania. The rest — Heniek and Olga, Szaja and Zygmunt, Sabina and her husband — turned back towards Warsaw.

6

Snow

JUST BEFORE MIDNIGHT, Natek, Zosia, Lolek and Danka got off a train in Soviet-occupied Poland near the Lithuanian border town of Eiszyszki. They were met by a Jewish guide they had hired through the grapevine of refugees before leaving Lvov. Guiding desperate people across the line had become a good source of income for poor peasants.

The little party started walking through open fields with snow up to their waists. It was a bright, clear night and the light of the moon bounced off the snow, illuminating the landscape. Every step was difficult and Zosia and Natek, who were considerably younger than Lolek and Danka, were soon some distance ahead of them and the guide. After a while, the newlyweds were confident that they had all crossed the border. Then Zosia and Natek heard dogs barking behind them and people shouting. They turned to see what was happening. Lolek, Danka and the guide had been caught by the Lithuanian police.

Scurrying to find a place to hide, Natek and Zosia struggled through the snow to a hiding place behind the nearest building and huddled there, shaking and gasping for air. The barking of the dogs was growing louder and Zosia was sure they would be tracked down. But eventually the noise stopped and she and Natek decided to look for a safer place to conceal themselves. If they stayed outside, they were bound to be seen in the moonlight. They noticed a shack nearby with a light in the window. "The owner might shelter us if we pay," Natek said.

They knocked on the door of the cottage. It was opened by a middle-aged peasant woman who seemed to be Jewish and spoke some Polish. She told them she lived alone. "Could we pay to stay for the night?" Natek asked. She said that would be fine and gave them some straw to sleep on. Exhausted from fear as well as their journey through the snow, Zosia and Natek dozed off immediately.

A knock at the door woke them. They held their breath and waited for the woman to answer it, but no one did, even as the knocking grew more intense. They realized that they were alone. "Zosia!" someone called from outside. "Natek!" They rose and opened the door. A young man they didn't recognize stood outside. "I've been sent to get you!" he panted. "You're not safe in this place. The police will come at any moment!"

They ran after him to another shack, where they were greeted by their guide as well as by Lolek and Danka, who looked shaken and pale.

"You're lucky I found out where you were," the guide said. "That woman whose house you were in is an informer. She has gone to get the police." He told Zosia and Natek how he had arranged Lolek and Danka's release: "Everyone has a scheme to make money out of this war, especially the patrol guards. They only care about lining their pockets."

"We had to give them everything," Lolek said. "They took our knapsacks and all of our clothes. All the gold I had is gone. I'll have to wire New York as soon as we get to Vilnius."

"The woman who offered you shelter will get a share of what they took from you," the guide, who was a Lithuanian Jew himself, explained to Lolek. "There are many Jews like her. They are a disgrace."

You must leave while it's still dark," the guide continued. "You will be too visible in daylight. If you're arrested again, the consequences could be more severe." He left them alone for half an hour, then returned in a horse-drawn sleigh. "This will take you all the way to Vilnius."

They paid the guide for his services, the driver cracked his whip, and the sleigh pulled away. It was -40° Celsius outside and, in the open sleigh, Zosia was convinced that even with her warm fur coat she would freeze to death. After a time on the way, they approached an inn with smoke spewing from its chimney.

"Let's go inside to warm up," she begged. "Just for a few minutes."

"It's much too dangerous!" Lolek told her.

Natek and Danka agreed with him. But Zosia was too cold and too tired.

"I'm freezing! I don't care if they find me!"

The others relented. They went in and sat down beside the fireplace, but a moment later the door opened and members of the Lithuanian border patrol swaggered in. The four Poles slipped out and jumped back into their sleigh. From then on, Zosia kept her grumbles to herself.

When they arrived in Vilnius early the next morning, cold and tired, they hurried into the first café they came to and asked for something to eat. The waitress came back with hard rolls and mouldy-looking jam, and they ate every morsel. Zosia felt it was the most wonderful meal she had ever eaten.

After their meal, they discovered that the narrow cobblestone streets were teeming with Jewish refugees. "It will be impossible to find accommodation," said Lolek. But then he had an idea. The main competitor of his family's business was a company called Original, and the owner lived in Vilnius. Lolek thought that this businessman might help them to find a place to live, so he made inquiries and learned his address. The others made themselves comfortable in a café and waited until Lolek came back. He returned sooner than they'd expected.

"The man was useless," he sighed. "He didn't even want to see me. When I explained who I was and why I'd come, he said, 'All of you Poles are lazy. You'd rather get drunk in Lithuania than be responsible citizens in Poland.'"

The four refugees walked around for hours. Eventually, they located a vacant room that was being sublet by a very poor middle-aged couple in a dilapidated building on Zawalna Street. This was one of the poorest parts of the city; the air smelled of sewage, and children in rags ran everywhere.

As they settled in, Zosia realized that she had never before been so close to poverty on a daily basis. And she admired some of what she saw. The local women supported their families by selling wares at the outdoor market, even in the bitterest cold, and Zosia marvelled at their ingenuity as the women kept warm by standing with their legs apart over hot bricks placed under their skirts.

Despite their miserable accommodation and her status as a refugee, Zosia was no longer depressed. The young bride loved and admired her new husband and, while she still missed her family, she was comforted to be with someone who valued her so much. Natek had a serious and determined nature, but he was also a passionate man, and the young couple glowed in the early throes of physical intimacy. They had little privacy, however, with Lolek and Danka sleeping on the other side of their shared room.

All over the city, Vilnius bubbled with the energy of the youthful Jewish refugees. There was a party atmosphere as the unemployed men and women filled the cafés and clubs, shared the latest rumours, and planned their next moves. It seemed to Zosia that the uncertainty of life enhanced everyone's enthusiasm for it. The vibrant cafés reminded her of Warsaw, and with Lolek, of course, there were always parties.

Lolek loved good food and, even in the owner's modest kitchen, Danka was able to supply it. Zosia had never had to clean or cook — she couldn't even boil a potato — and was astonished both by Danka's culinary skills and her willingness to do anything for Lolek. She even polished his shoes! Once, while Danka was asleep, he asked her for a cup of tea, and she rose as if in a trance, put on the kettle, made him tea, and immediately fell back asleep. It was as if he had pretty Danka under some sort of spell.

Both Bluman brothers loved to play bridge and other refugees joined them for games in their broken-down room, with Lolek shouting and screaming if his partner made a mistake. For the most part, though, Natek, who was increasingly desperate to reach the United States, tirelessly strategized their escape. He cabled Mr. Catz, who was unable to help with visas but did provide access to Natek's American bank account.

Almost daily, Natek took the train to Kaunas and trudged from embassy to embassy in search of the visas that would get them out of Europe. No countries were interested in taking Jews, however, and day after day he came home looking disheartened. Sometimes Zosia went with him, and they usually spent part of their time in Kaunas in a café called the Monika, which was popular among the refugees.

Polish Jews were still flooding into Lithuania, full of news about what was going on in Warsaw. The reports were not good. It was rumoured that a Jewish ghetto had already been established. People were being forced out of their homes and were disappearing from the streets. Zosia felt helpless so far away from her family. She remembered the day when the German soldiers had pulled Symcha around by his beard.

One afternoon, Natek returned to Vilnius after a particularly frustrating day of being turned away from embassy after embassy in Kaunas, only to be greeted by Zosia with her face awash in tears.

"I'm pregnant!" she said.

Natek embraced his young wife, but his arms were stiff.

"We must do something about it," he said, trying to sound matter-of-fact. "We cannot move freely with a child. And we have barely enough money to support ourselves. How will we support a baby?"

But she could already feel the child developing within her.

"I want to have it!"

"It makes no sense; it would be a disaster!" Natek insisted, his temper rising. "No one wants to give us a visa now. Do you think it will be easier with a baby?"

They argued all through the night. Zosia suggested a variety of ways to make the situation work, but eventually she had to agree that Natek's concerns were legitimate. Relieved, Natek urged her to speak to Danka. Zosia raised the matter in the morning, and Danka reassured her. "Don't worry," she said. "I've had several abortions. You'll be fine."

Zosia underwent the procedure in a clean, well-staffed clinic. Although they knew their decision was realistic, a sense of loss darkened the lives of the young couple. And Natek's money was running out. He anxiously looked for work but had as little success finding a job as he'd had finding a visa. Then one day as he was walking through Vilnius, he bumped into an instructor he'd had at the Agricultural University of Warsaw. Professor Szpilfogel was a refugee now too, and was overjoyed to see one of his prize pupils. Natek told him that he was becoming discouraged looking for employment.

"You're in luck," Professor Szpilfogel said. "I have the perfect job for you if you are willing to live in Keydany. You don't know it? A small village a hundred kilometres from here. There is a community of young Zionists there, and they asked if I knew anyone who could teach them about farming. They'll need to know such things when they get to Palestine."

"I would be very interested," said Natek. "My wife and I would have no problem moving to Keydany."

"Then the job is yours," Professor Szpilfogel smiled. "I will make the arrangements. You should go as soon as possible."

Natek ran home to tell Zosia the good news. She tried to look pleased.

"But are you sure that there is no job for you in Vilnius?"

"I've looked everywhere! There is nothing."

"I've never lived in the country," Zosia said. Especially in this time of grief, she didn't want to leave the vitality and friendliness of Vilnius for the boredom and loneliness of rural life.

"We have no choice," Natek replied.

Zosia couldn't deny that the money would be helpful. "I suppose we ought to take advantage of the opportunity," she finally agreed.

They left for Keydany in April 1940. They said their goodbyes to Lolek and Danka, then rode a series of buses to a kibbutz called Hashomer Hatzazier. It was nothing more than a row of huts built on the edge of the fields tilled by the kibbutzniks. Fifty Zionists shared the huts. All were similar in age to Zosia and Natek, but none were married.

The next day, Natek and Zosia were invited to stay on the kibbutz permanently. Natek, who was impressed with communal living and with the kibbutz itself, tried to convince Zosia to accept the invitation. But this time she put her foot down. She had never been a Zionist and felt nothing in common with the idealistic kibbutzniks. She hadn't liked it when they tried to make her join in the Jewish folk dancing — that was not the kind of dancing she had enjoyed in Warsaw — and she particularly hated eating in the communal dining room. "I will not stay here," she said, leaving no room for discussion.

In the nearby village, Natek found a shack that was inhabited by a Jewish family named Parkus. The building had no plumbing and consisted of one room and a kitchen. The family of five lived in the kitchen. Natek and Zosia rented the other room.

Shortly after their arrival in Keydany, Natek received a postcard from his brother Zygmunt, who had returned to Warsaw with Heniek and Olga. Natek had written to him asking for the family business's pickle recipe. Zygmunt's reply was an odd mixture of practicality and barely suppressed anxiety.

"For the brine, use 150 kg of water boiled and then cooled, 2 kg of vinegar, 8 kg of salt, 320 grams of benzoic acid," he wrote. But he also confessed: "I intended to go to Krakow and, at that time, I liquidated everything. It was a big mistake and stupid and I can't forgive myself. I am very sorry but there is nothing I can do." What did he mean? Had he dissolved the company? In a postscript, he added, "I am surprised that Lolek is angry at me for some unknown reasons. In order to understand me, he has to be in my situation." What situation? What couldn't Zygmunt bring himself to say? There was one clue: the return address indicated that Zygmunt had moved, which seemed to confirm the rumour that the Jews of Warsaw had been confined to a ghetto.

Family and home have always been of the utmost importance to my parents.

When Drew and I married on May 24, 1978, I was pregnant with our first son, Michael, who was born in October. Two other children came quickly: Danielle in March of 1980, and Sam in April of 1983.

We were living in a house on Quesnel Street in the Dunbar neighbourhood of Vancouver. And, in early 1980, when I was pregnant with Danielle, Drew and I bought another very significant property.

As soon as I saw the beach house on Indian Arm, which is an inlet north of Vancouver, I felt as though I were home. This came as a surprise to Drew, who loved the place himself, but thought I wouldn't be impressed. As he put it, Manhattan was more my idea of paradise. But my heart settled as soon as I walked into that little cabin in the bush.

We were less sure of ourselves the day we first took possession. We faced real west coast winter weather as we drove towards the beach house along a road that slithers up and down the side of Seymour Mountain: it was pouring with rain. Drew's dad Frank and his stepmother Diane had come over from Victoria to be with us, and my parents had come along, too.

When we opened the door, it almost fell off its hinges. Rain was streaming in through the roof. Not a single light would turn on. Drew and I exchanged looks that asked, "What have we done?" How could we ever get our money back on this reckless purchase?

But our two sets of parents said, "Oh, come on! Don't be such babies. Let's get at it." And we all started cleaning up.

After that, Mom and Dad came out to the beach house often. My father worked hard out there. My folks would sleep over and, every day, my dad would have his breakfast and then get on with a morning project.

At the cabin, if you stand in the kitchen looking out at the water, you see wooden doors with glass panes that go out onto the deck.

At some point, somebody had painted over the glass. Over many months, Dad cleaned every single pane of glass with a razor blade.

After he had finished his morning task and he'd had his lunch, he would set up his reel-to-reel tape recorder, lie down on the beaten up old couch we'd gotten at an auction, pull an old blanket over himself, and listen to the tapes he'd made of the CBC Radio Orchestra.

In the summer afternoons, Drew was almost always down by the water playing with the kids, all of them brown as nuts.

From the time that Sammy was very little, he would become sick if he thought that an animal was being hurt. His older siblings knew this, of course. The blackberry brambles next door to the beach house were full of garter snakes. One day, as I was suntanning on the deck with my mother, I heard Sam screaming. When I looked down, his brother Michael was holding a snake, not hurting it, but threatening to. Before I could intervene, Drew was there. Michael dropped the snake. He knew when he was in trouble. Drew told Michael to knock it off and reassured Sam.

I looked over at my mother. She loved watching Drew with the kids. ✖

In the isolation of Keydany, Zosia allowed herself to fall into a kind of ease. In the dull countryside, she was pleasantly insulated from the daily reports of war. She heard only rumours and most of those were stale. She felt little of the panic that gripped other areas of the world when Germany invaded Belgium, Holland and Luxembourg, and she could only dimly imagine the ominous calm that set in after they fell. She heard about the British evacuation of Dunkirk, but events on the English Channel were far away from their lives with the Parkus family and the kibbutzniks. News that the German army had entered Paris was surprising and worrisome, but Zosia felt removed from it. It was quiet in Keydany and, with the arrival of spring, almost pretty. She worried about her family, but there was nothing she could do. Absolutely nothing.

During all this time, Natek remained obsessed with getting out of Europe, and he knew that to do so he would have to think three steps ahead. Zosia did not have a passport, which meant that she might not be able to leave Lithuania. Fortunately, on one of his visits to Kaunas, Natek had learned that the British consul acted as the representative of the Polish government-in-exile and had the authority to add his wife's name to his passport.

But this posed another problem because, in order to get Zosia onto his passport, Natek needed proof of marriage. When he and Zosia had wed in Lvov, it had been a purely religious wedding. The Soviet government did not recognize religious ceremonies and so did not issue a marriage certificate. Although Zosia and Natek were willing to remarry, Jewish law prohibited a rabbi from conducting a second ceremony.

They suffered a great deal of worry and frustration before a lawyer friend in Keydany found them a rabbi who was prepared to ignore this rule for a fee. The second marriage was hastily performed, the rabbi issued the certificate, and Natek and Zosia went immediately to the British consulate and had the matter sorted out. Days later, on June 14, 1940, the Soviets invaded Lithuania. If Natek had waited, adding Zosia's name to his passport would have been impossible.

For Natek, and increasingly for Zosia, this small victory was overwhelmed by a feeling of impending doom. With the Soviets on the move, everyone agreed that Germany and the Soviet Union would soon be at war. The only way out was to the east, but that required more documents: they would need an exit visa to leave Lithuania and a transit visa to cross the Soviet Union. Natek continued to try to obtain visas in Kaunas but embassies were clamping down tighter all the time. And, once Germany and the Soviet Union were at war, even this faint possibility of escape would be extinguished. As Zosia awoke from her slumber, she found herself in a situation that seemed hopeless.

7

A Maze Made of Paper

ALTHOUGH ZOSIA AND NATEK didn't know it, a young Dutchman was opening a door that they would soon be struggling to
enter.

In July 1940, a Dutch student at a Lithuanian *yeshiva*, or Jewish
theological school, sought the assistance of Jan Zwartendijk, the
businessman who was serving as honorary Dutch consul. The
Netherlands was already under German occupation and, as was
the case with Zosia and Natek, the Dutchman's goal was to get out
of Europe as quickly as possible. He had heard that Zwartendijk
was sympathetic to the plight of Jewish refugees, but he wasn't
sure how much he could trust him, so he began by telling the consul that he wanted to find a way to return to the Netherlands so
that he could see his family.

"Can you help me?" he asked Zwartendijk.

"Do you have any ideas?"

The student was certain that, if he could get an entry document to any destination not under German occupation, he would be able to acquire the other two documents he needed: an exit visa out of Lithuania and a transit visa through the Soviet Union. In other words, if he could prove that he would be allowed to enter a place such as the Dutch island of Curaçao, it was more likely that he would be allowed to leave Lithuania and travel across the Soviet Union. Getting the entry document was the crucial first step in his plan. That's what he asked Zwartendijk for.

"What about endorsing my passport to say that I am eligible for admission to Curaçao, in the Dutch West Indies? I don't think Curaçao requires a visa."

"But you need the governor's permission to enter Curaçao. It's seldom given."

"But, sir," said the young man, "do you think anyone needs to know that?"

"Hand me your passport," said Zwartendijk.

He printed, "For Curaçao, no visa is required." He did not add the additional sentence required by consular protocol: "Only the local governor has the authority to issue landing permits."

"I think," he said, "this will provide you what you need."

"Thank you, sir." The young man took the passport back. "Now I was wondering if you could give me advice on one other matter."

"And what is that?"

The student wanted to get to Japan. From there, he could achieve his ultimate goal, which was to travel to somewhere safe, such as North America or Palestine. "I don't think that it's possible to go directly to Curaçao from the Soviet Union, and I will likely get stuck in Vladivostok," he began. "However, I have looked at a map and it seems that if I take the Trans-Siberian Railroad from

Natek Bluman teaching students at a Zionist colony in Keydany
(near Vilnius, Lithuania), May 1940. Natek is standing on the far right.

Natek Bluman's Polish passport photo

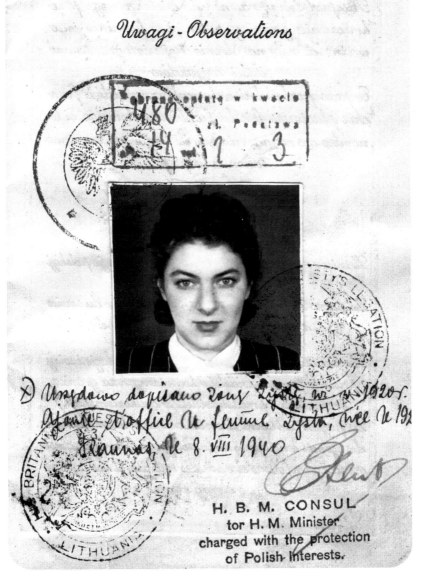

Natek had Zosia added to his Polish passport by the British Consul in Kaunas, Lithuania, in 1940, an act that made it possible for them to leave Lithuania.

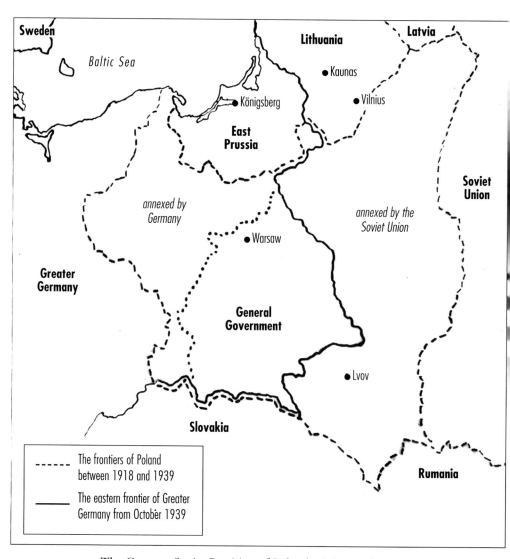

The German-Soviet Partition of Poland, 28 September 1939

Chiune Sugihara at his desk. As the Japanese Consul
in Kaunas, Lithuania, Sugihara saved the lives of upwards
of six thousand Jewish refugees by issuing them
travel visas — against the orders of his superiors. He
was awarded the title of "Righteous Gentile."

PHOTO CREDIT: *Visas for Life Foundation*

Jewish refugees waiting outside the gates of the Japanese
Consulate in Kaunas, Lithuania, c. 1940.
PHOTO CREDIT: *Visas for Life Foundation*

Chiune Sugihara and his wife Yukiko, who supported him in his decision to disobey orders and issue travel visas to Jewish refugees.

Chiune Sugihara and Yukiko standing in front of a wire fence.
The sign in German translates as "Entry denied to Jews."
PHOTO CREDIT: *Visas for Life Foundation*

Moscow to Vladivostok, it would only be a short journey by ship to Japan. What are my chances of getting a transit visa that would allow me to land in that country?"

Zwartendijk nodded at the young man.

"I have met the Japanese consul. I think that he might be willing to help you."

Zwartendijk knew Chiune Sugihara, the Japanese consul, to be a cosmopolitan man. Sugihara had completed his diplomatic studies in Harbin, in Japanese-controlled China and, after graduation, he had climbed quickly through the ranks of the Japanese foreign ministry there. Harbin was a racially diverse city — it even had a Jewish community — and, while living there, Sugihara converted to Christianity and married a Belarusian woman named Klaudia, although they divorced ten years later.

In a remarkable move, he resigned a later diplomatic post in occupied Manchuria to protest Japanese cruelty to the Chinese.

But Zwartendijk also knew that Sugihara would be hard-pressed to help the student, even if he wanted to. His Japanese masters would never allow him to do anything that might upset Japan's increasingly important alignment with anti-Semitic Germany.

Consul Sugihara asked the Dutchman about his plans.

"Sir, I intend to go to Curaçao," the student lied. "I have no intention of staying in Japan," he added, telling the truth.

Consul Sugihara examined his passport. He studied Zwartendijk's endorsement and satisfied himself that the young man indeed intended to go to Curaçao. He saw no reason to deny him the visa that would allow him to enter Japan, and issued him one.

Armed with his Curaçao endorsement and Japanese transit visa, the young man went to the Soviet authorities and was issued both an exit visa from Lithuania and the transit visa that would allow him to cross the USSR. Every step had fallen into place. There was a way out.

Isolated in Keydany, Zosia and Natek heard nothing of this but, amongst the refugees in Kaunas, rumours about the Dutch student's visas circulated quickly, and Jews began visiting Zwartendijk. He endorsed the passport of every refugee who came to see him. He advised all of them to visit the Japanese consulate so that they could sail to Japan once they had crossed the Soviet Union.

In the beginning, while word was only beginning to spread, only a trickle of refugees made their way to the Japanese consulate, and Consul Sugihara, carefully applying Foreign Ministry protocol, issued them transit visas. At first he did not seem unduly concerned about the substantial increase in the number of people who claimed each to be headed for Curaçao, an island off the Venezuelan coast.

Then, on the morning of July 26, 1940, Sugihara was awakened by a raucous noise outside the consulate, and was astounded to see a ragtag mob of refugees clutching at the gates. He was so stunned that he picked up his camera and took photographs of the bizarre sight. He called to his wife Yukiko and she came running, along with their son Hiroki. Standing at the window, they stared at the men, women and children pushing and shoving to get into the consulate. Their clothes were dishevelled, and their eyes desperate.

"Who are those people?" asked Yukiko.

Now, Sugihara understood. He had met Jews in Harbin who had left Germany to escape oppression. "They are Jews who want visas so that they can get out of Europe," he said. "They believe they will be killed if the Nazis invade Lithuania."

"Is that likely?" she asked.

"It is possible."

Five-year-old Hiroki could not stop staring at a young boy

whose fingers were wound around the bars of the gate. The boy's face was dirty and his eyes half-open. "Will you help them?" Hiroki asked his father.

Sugihara did not know what to say. Although he was aware of the virulence of Nazi anti-Semitism, he had not been prepared for this onslaught of refugees. After all, it was his job to inform the Japanese government about the situation in Germany and Eastern Europe, and the persecution of the Jews had been the subject of many of his reports.

While Sugihara shared his son's sympathy for the refugees' predicament, he could not let his actions be dictated simply by emotion. He had to consider his career and his family's safety. He had recently been ordered to report to the Japanese embassy in Berlin; in fact, he would be in Germany in less than three weeks.

But Sugihara could not, in all conscience, keep the gates locked. He let it be known that five people could come to his office as representatives of the crowd. Zwartendijk came in with the five Jews selected, and the consul politely welcomed the delegation.

"Why is there such a big crowd at my gate?"

The representatives explained that everyone at the gate was in grave danger if they remained in Lithuania. The other European countries had refused to help and now, with the Germans on the move, they could only hope to escape Europe by going east.

"Honourable Consul Sugihara," Zwartendijk said, "I have endorsed their passports so that they can go to Curaçao. Unfortunately, they have no way of getting there without first landing in Japan. I told them that you are a compassionate man and would assist by issuing transit visas."

Now Sugihara was suspicious.

"Will they be welcomed in Curaçao?"

Zwartendijk saw there was no point continuing with the fiction.

"Honourable Consul Sugihara," he said, "none of these people plan to go to Curaçao. These Jews are only concerned with getting out of Europe. They are desperate. The Nazis have occupied Western Europe, and they will soon move east. In my own country, Jews are being rounded up and persecuted. You and I are uniquely able to help them."

"It would be impossible to issue visas that would allow them to live permanently in Japan."

One of the Jewish representatives spoke up. He was an American who had been sent to Europe by the Palestine-based Jewish Agency. "Honourable Consul Sugihara, you have my assurance that the refugees will not stay in Japan," he said. "The Jewish Agency will find safe havens for all those who reach your country. I can also assure you that they will not pose a financial burden on Japan, as funds to support the refugees have already been raised in the United States."

Sugihara thanked the delegates for their thoughtful presentations. As he showed them out of his office, he told them that he would consider their request.

The representatives left the consulate more than satisfied; they had had a good hearing. Conditions in Lithuania were deteriorating and hope was in very short supply — by this point, Japan's was the only consulate the Soviets had allowed to stay open — so the crowd cheered as the representatives reported that the consul had not turned them down outright.

The next morning, the crowd had grown even larger. The line of refugees curved away from the gate like an anxious snake and the noise was overwhelming.

Sugihara realized that he could not make this decision on his own. There were broad foreign policy consequences. The refugees would have to wait a few more hours while he cabled the Foreign Ministry in Tokyo for permission.

Although Natek and Zosia were still unaware of this unfolding drama, Lolek and Danka had joined the line at Zwartendijk's office.

Finally, Sugihara received a response to his cable: the Japanese Foreign Ministry did not want to take any action that might undermine Japan's increasingly important relations with Germany.

As he read the cable, Sugihara could hear the crowd outside. He looked out at the mass of faces. He was not a sentimental man, but how could he ignore them? He decided that a second request was in order, and this time he took care to explain why he felt that they ought to help these people leave Europe. He assured the Foreign Ministry that he would give the Jews transit visas only; they would not stay in Japan.

But permission to issue the visas was again denied. When he tried a third time, the reply included the line, "No further inquiries expected."

Sugihara consulted Yukiko. "My superiors in Tokyo cannot expect me to dishonour my country and my emperor, and turn away from desperate people," he said.

"I will stand by you," Yukiko told him, "if you do what is right."

Even though they feared for Sugihara's career, the family's financial future and even their lives and those of their children, they decided to follow their consciences.

So on July 27, 1940, the Honourable Consul Sugihara started to write visas. For each one, he registered the name of the recipient in his ledger along with their nationality and the date of issue. He worked day and night. On July 31, 1940, Lolek and Danka entered the office of Consul Sugihara and requested transit visas, and Sugihara recorded in his ledger that recipient number 515 was Danuta Lapacz and number 516 was Szoel-Leopold Bluman. They had received two of the 144 visas issued that day.

8

Suffocation and Breath

AFTER THEY MOVED TO Keydany, Zosia and Natek seldom heard from Lolek. He had no interest in leaving the comforts of the big city, and he could not understand how Natek could isolate himself on a kibbutz. "You're not a farmer!" he scoffed.

So, at the beginning of August, Zosia and Natek were especially surprised to receive a visit from Lolek.

"Pack up!" he said. Then, to their astonishment, he opened his passport to reveal a strange eastern script. "It's Japanese," he explained. "The Japanese consul is giving a visa to anyone who asks. We can go to the United States from Japan!"

Zosia was stunned. She had learned about Japan years before in school, but was no longer sure of where it was located. Lolek explained the Dutch student's scheme to her and Natek and urged them to be quick about capitalizing on his success. "I suggest you go as soon as possible," he said. "Who knows how many visas the Japanese consulate will give out? Danka and I received ours a week ago. There were long line-ups even then. And now everyone knows about this."

"Then we won't wait!" said Natek. "I'll go to the kibbutz and tell them I have to leave immediately."

Leaving Keydany with Natek, Zosia was aware of a new fear: the fear of hoping for too much. And, as they approached the office of the honorary Dutch consul in Kaunas, clutching their shared precious passport, that fear grew. They were surprised to see no sign of the line of people that Lolek had described and, when they reached the door, they discovered why. It was locked. Zwartendijk had obviously vacated the premises; they assumed that he had fled the approaching Germans.

Zosia could feel her heart burning, and she saw that Natek's face was blotched with red spots. "Why did Lolek wait so long to tell us?" he spat out. "Weeks! I can never rely on him!" Zosia kept her hand on his shoulder and remained silent. Even if a person could manage to obtain a transit visa to Japan, it was useless without an entry visa to a final destination such as Curaçao. They were trapped and they fell silent.

"But perhaps we can use my American visa!" Natek suddenly exclaimed, turning towards Zosia. "It has expired, but the Soviets may not realize that. After all, they do not speak English, so we may be able to convince them that we would be granted permission to enter the US. And we might really be able to get my visa extended at the American embassy in Japan."

Zosia felt her throat constrict. Ever since Lolek's news had put getting out of Europe within their grasp, she had become increasingly desperate to escape. Natek was her family now, and she felt so grateful to be with such an intelligent and resourceful man. If he had not had the foresight to add her name to his passport, she wouldn't have a chance now of escaping to America.

"Yes," she said. "Why not?"

They walked to the Japanese consulate, which was on a bright street in a fashionable part of Kaunas. They saw a line of people in front of a white, three-storey structure, and took their places at the end.

As they waited, the hours dragged like days. Then, when it was finally their turn, Zosia was too nervous to go inside. She knew that this was only the first of a number of precarious steps. Natek went into the consulate to speak for both of them.

Waiting outside, she alternated between calm and panic. Finally, Natek came out the door with his arms outstretched. "We got it!" he shouted as he grabbed her and hugged her.

At the same time, Chiune Sugihara pulled out his register and wrote that on August 9, 1940, transit visa number 1569 had been issued to Natek Bluman.

Without a final destination visa for Curaçao, Natek and Zosia slept uneasily as they prepared themselves for their next hurdle: obtaining an exit visa from the Soviets. Their only hope was that the authorities would believe Natek's story about the American visa being extended, though he and Zosia could not ignore the rumours that those denied exit visas were being exiled to Siberia.

Lolek harboured no such fears. Armed with his Curaçao endorsement and Japanese transit visa, he went to the Soviet consulate and returned smiling. "They said that we should have our visas in about two weeks," he declared.

Zosia felt too nervous to meet the Soviet authorities with her husband. "Please, Natek," she said, "you go alone and speak for both of us, as you did at the Japanese consulate." But he wanted her to come. "I always have better luck when you are with me," he insisted. Again, Zosia said that the interview would be more than she could bear, and Natek turned away, looking tired. Zosia had always felt that Natek was so good at making plans and getting things done that she had little to offer, but maybe he really did need her to stand beside him now. "All right," she said, "I'll come," and she saw the gratitude in her husband's face.

To bulk up her courage she reminded herself that she had lived through a blitzkrieg, the Nazi occupation and two days' confinement by Russian soldiers. When she considered all of that, going into an office building, even a Soviet one, was a little less daunting.

As they walked towards the Soviet consulate, they discussed their situation for the hundredth time, and agreed that whatever fate awaited them at the hands of the Soviets paled in comparison to what was being faced by Polish Jews under German occupation. They had no doubt now that the Jews of Warsaw had been confined to a ghetto. Letters from the family didn't say as much — perhaps their relatives wanted to spare them worry — but there were too many reports to deny the existence of the ghetto now. They had even heard that Natek's father had not returned home after leaving Lvov so many months before. "Deportation to Siberia is no worse than going back," Natek said, "and no worse than waiting for the Nazis to march into Lithuania."

The young couple entered the Soviet consulate and, to their surprise and relief, the official they met was pleasant. They were able to communicate with him using their broken Yiddish, and Zosia wondered if he might be Jewish.

He studied their passport carefully.

"Where are you going? I see a transit visa to Japan but no final destination."

"Please look more closely, sir," Natek said, keeping his voice steady. "I have a visa to the United States. I was there last year. The visa can be extended but there is no American consulate in Kaunas.

Once I reach a consulate I will be able to have it extended."

"Are you sure?" the official asked.

"Oh, yes. I am sure it can be extended at the American embassy in Moscow," Natek answered confidently.

The man looked sceptical.

"Perhaps you are right, but I must check. Leave your passport with me and, if it's possible this can be extended, I will issue an exit visa."

Zosia could barely breathe as they walked out of the consulate. Natek's face was ashen. Although they had been hoping to have their American visa extended in Japan, they both knew that it would be impossible to get it extended in Moscow. Their precious passport was in the hands of the Soviets and they were sure that they would never see it again. "We will never get to America," Natek muttered over and over.

Since they no longer had a home in Keydany, they returned to Lolek and Danka's in Vilnius. A week passed and then another with no word from the Soviets.

Finally, they received a letter asking them to return to the consulate. They suspected that they were in serious trouble. Lolek and Danka had applied for their exit visas prior to them but had not yet heard anything, so being called in ahead of Lolek and his girl-friend felt ominous. But they couldn't run away — they had no passport — and they resigned themselves to facing whatever the Soviets had in store.

After they got off the bus in Kaunas, their feet dragged them towards the consulate. Zosia's mouth was dry, her breath felt stale, and her stomach kept turning. She had not been able to eat properly for days.

They were greeted by the same Yiddish-speaking official. They stood at the counter, gave him their names, and explained that they had applied two weeks earlier for an exit visa. The official smiled.

"Yes, I remember you." He pulled out Natek's passport from a drawer. "Your exit visa has been approved. Everything is in order. You will have to go to Intourist to make your travel arrangements. I hope you have a safe trip."

He held out the passport and Natek took it, though his hands shook so violently that he could barely hold it. At first, Zosia thought she'd misunderstood the man but now that Natek had the passport, she realized that she'd heard correctly.

Once outside the consulate, Natek and Zosia were too relieved, too spent, to feel ecstatic. Zosia was shivering and drenched with perspiration. If their luck continued to hold, they were going to Japan — not the gulag. As Natek embraced her, Zosia felt proud that they had defied the odds, and they'd done it together.

The next day, they went to the Intourist office to make their travel arrangements. Making a reservation on the train was difficult because of the war, and they were told that, even though it was still summer, seats could not be found until the end of the year at the earliest. Natek said that they would take the first reservation available.

The tickets had to be purchased in precious American dollars and, even by pre-war standards, the price was exorbitant, but Natek had heard about the high cost and had come prepared. As he handed the official the money, Zosia thought again how fortunate they were.

"Now," the official added, "I will require 300 American dollars to cover the cost of the food you will receive on the train."

The young couple was dumbfounded. It was more than they could afford to pay. In fact, it was enough money to feed the two of them for a year!

"Sir," said Natek, "we had not realized. If you please, we will bring our own food along. We're not fussy."

"You cannot bring your own food on the train. You must pay

the $300 in advance or I cannot sell you the tickets."

As they left the Intourist office, Zosia felt faint with disappointment. Against all odds, they had obtained the necessary papers, and now found themselves trapped in Lithuania because they did not have enough American dollars to pay for their meals.

Over the next week, Natek tried to raise the money they needed, but it proved impossible to acquire that much American cash. Each day, Hitler seemed closer to invading England, and Natek told Zosia that it seemed certain that the Nazis would arrive in Lithuania before they'd be able to get away. If that happened, all of their efforts since leaving Warsaw would be in vain, and they'd be thrown into a ghetto like all the others.

Natek was a dignified man but, to save himself and his young wife, he was willing to beg. "I must go back to Intourist and convince them to let us bring our own food," he said. "And I want you to come with me. You give me good luck."

They were met by the same man at the Intourist office. Natek explained that they were simply unable to pay $300.

"Please let us bring our own food," he pleaded.

"I cannot do that," the official replied tersely. "You are required to pay in advance for the meals. That is the rule."

Natek tried to bargain but the official remained resistant, and Zosia felt more and more desperate. Finally, she could not control herself any longer and began to cry. Once the tears had started, they flowed freely down her face.

The agent looked at her, startled. Then he turned back to Natek.

"How much American money do you have?"

"I have $100, sir."

"Give me fifty and keep the rest."

They gave the man the $50 and thanked him profusely. As the agent handed their tickets across, he informed the young couple that he had reserved two seats for them on a train to the Soviet Union, departing at the beginning of January, 1941. But that was months away, plenty of time for the tense relationship between the USSR and Germany to descend into war.

≈ My parents were relentless in their struggle for survival — especially my father.

That tenacity has a dark side. After the war, my father's determination solidified into painful rigidity. He became a respected biochemist in the Canadian Health Protection Branch, but he was scarred by the war. He was not a man who found it easy to express his feelings, he did not have close friends, and it wasn't unusual for his bitterness to spew forth in vitriolic anger. When I was a small child, I would hide whenever he was in one of his moods and, as a teenager, I would retreat to the home of a girlfriend, sometimes sleeping over for nights at a time.

I inherited some of that tenacity.

Just as my father used to disappear into dark moods or into the basement to listen to Rachmaninoff, my husband Drew disappeared into our living room where he often spent evenings in front of the fireplace with the lights out, smoking cigarettes and drinking whiskey.

I didn't ignore the issue, but I was determined to keep my marriage alive.

Our fighting must have affected the kids, however. I remember one night when Drew came home late smelling of alcohol. When I asked him where he'd been, he got defensive and before long we were screaming at each other. Danielle, who was eight at the time, came padding out of her bedroom in her pyjamas and asked us if everything was all right.

Drew's drinking never became an issue outside of our immediate family. Even my parents and brothers didn't know about it.

For me, the biggest blow was when Drew told me that he'd had an affair. Our children were still very young — Michael was five, Danielle was four, and Sam was a baby — when Drew told me that he'd been seeing a woman named Janet and that he'd fathered a child with her, a daughter named Jamie. He insisted that the relationship was over, that he had never intended to leave me, and that he wanted to stay. Still, he couldn't have shocked or hurt me more. At first, I felt like I couldn't breathe. Later, my whole body felt bruised.

Michelle, Danielle and Sam weren't told about their half-sister until about twelve years later.

We were at our place on Indian Arm. He sat the children down at the kitchen table and laid out the story. I remember the kids sitting there with their heads down, not knowing what to say. Finally, Mike asked, "Can we go now?" We said they could.

After Drew and I split up, Danielle told me that she and her brothers didn't say a word to one another about what they'd been told. ≈

9

A Ride in the Dark

≈ Maybe it shouldn't have come as a shock to me when Drew left for good, but it did. And, when he left, it was as though he flicked a switch and, all of a sudden, he had never loved me. When he came to pick up the kids, he looked at me as though he'd never seen me before.

He had met another woman. She was also a lawyer.

I felt as if I'd been pushed out of an airplane. I didn't have a parachute and, for the next year, I just kept falling.

The cancer that I'm fighting now is a breeze compared to the end of my marriage.

I tried to go on working, but I kept collapsing into myself. By this time, I had become quite a high-profile arbitrator. I enjoyed being called to the far reaches of the province to apply my skills. Now, I'd get phone calls saying, "We're all here, sitting around the table. Where are you?" I was terrified that word would get out, my practice would dissolve, and I would be unable to pay my bills.

My mother has always gathered the whole family at her house for dinner on Sunday nights. All of us, even the grandchildren's friends, squeeze around her small dining room table. Drew and I had attended regularly with our kids.

I found my first Sunday dinner without my husband so difficult that I had to excuse myself from the table. I went downstairs and cried. My mother came down after me.

"I can't believe that my daughter could be so weak," she told me. "Lots of women have gone through a divorce. Surely you can handle it. How can you cry in front of your children? I never cried in front of you or your brothers, even after everything I have been through." ⊰≋⊱

The precarious balance between Germany and the Soviet Union held and, in January, Zosia and Natek carried all of their belongings to the station and boarded the train. Lolek and Danka would follow later; they had waited six long weeks before receiving their exit visas.

Natek and Zosia had one suitcase between them, containing a pillow and a few clothes. The precious money belt that Symcha had given her was firmly buckled around Zosia's waist. It had effectively hidden the little cash she had carried over many months of flight; Zosia couldn't leave it behind now. And she wore the fur-lined coat that had already served her so well from Warsaw to Lvov to Vilnius.

Once on board, and the train had begun clattering across the Soviet Union, Zosia felt her jaw begin to unclench and the knot in her stomach begin to relax. The further away she got from the Nazis, the safer she felt.

After two days they reached Moscow, where they were to wait three days before catching another train to take them all the way across the USSR.

They knew only one person in this sombre city, and decided to visit her. She was a childhood friend of Natek's mother, a committed Communist who had moved to the Soviet Union as a girl to pursue her political dream. Natek's mother had given him her address before he left Warsaw, in the event that he ever found himself in the Soviet Union. Natek managed to make contact and she invited the young couple to visit her.

Zosia and Natek hailed a taxi and gave the driver the address. He dropped them off in front of a once-regal apartment building that now looked grim. They walked down many corridors, searching the long lists of names on the apartment doors. Finally, they found the woman's door and she let them in. Her quarters consisted of one tiny room.

"It is so good to see you, Natek," she said. "And such a pleasure to meet your pretty wife. How did you get here?"

"We took a taxi," Zosia replied.

The woman's face turned white.

"A taxi? The driver will know you came to see me!"

"We're sorry," Natek said. "We did not realize."

"We are not allowed any contact with foreigners," she answered, her eyes darting towards the hallway.

Zosia opened her pack and handed the woman a few of the clothes and other belongings that they had brought from Lithuania. The woman relaxed a little and told them that she was very grateful. She went to a cabinet and brought out a single orange. Her hands quivered as she peeled. She carefully cut it into twenty pieces and shared them with her guests.

"This is a terrible place to live," she confided. "You are lucky that you can leave. I wish I were going with you. Everyone wants to leave, just like me. Everyone is scared."

After a short visit, the woman apologetically told the couple that they had to go. "It is too dangerous, you must not stay longer. And please be more discreet on the way out. I will be in trouble if they find out you were at my apartment."

Zosia and Natek had already been afraid of being watched. Now, back at their hotel, they were even more worried. Convinced that their room was bugged, they climbed under their covers and spoke in whispers.

After three uneasy days, they packed their bags and headed back to the station. Their new train was surprisingly comfortable. The cars were heated, the seats were padded, and there were porters and a dining car. They could not afford to eat there, but having a dining car was reassuring, nonetheless. Everything seemed so *normal*.

It was a long trip — eleven days — and Zosia and Natek were always wary. They spoke quietly and were careful not to say anything that could be interpreted as anti-Soviet.

At one of the last stops before Vladivostok, Zosia excitedly grabbed Natek's arm and pointed out the window. "Look! That sign is in Yiddish!" Other Jewish refugees had noticed the same thing and there was a rush of whispered astonishment. Then, as the door opened, they could hear someone outside speaking in the familiar Jewish tongue. The woman sitting in front of Zosia turned around. "We're in Birobidzhan," she said. "Stalin wants to make it a Jewish state of the USSR. Lots of Jews have been *asked* to relocate here."

Finally, they arrived in Vladivostok. They were told that, because of wartime security measures, they could not leave the train in such an important port until after dark. So they waited three hours until night fell. The city became silent, and it darkened until the only light was from the pale glow of the stars. Under the cover of night, the passengers were marched to waiting buses, which took them to the docks. Zosia could see nothing as they drove along; the windows were blacked out. Then the bus stopped and they were guided onto a Japanese ship that was waiting in the harbour.

Because they had so little money, Zosia and Natek had booked passage in the lowest class, which meant sleeping on mats at the bottom of the ship with the other third-class passengers, all of whom were Japanese. At first, Zosia was taken aback to be sharing quarters with people who looked odd to her, but she noticed that the Japanese seemed equally surprised to be travelling with Europeans.

The journey to Japan took two days. All her life, Zosia had suffered from motion sickness and, crossing those stormy seas, she became violently seasick and vomited constantly. The Japanese passengers tried to comfort her. A young woman with a warm smile offered her an apple, and then others offered what food they had. Zosia politely declined, but the kindness gave her hope. Maybe Jews would truly be welcome in Japan.

Still, any sort of food just made her ever more sick, and soon she had nothing more to retch. She worried that somehow she was letting Natek down, but all she could do was give in to the nausea. And there was another kind of pain mixed in with her physical misery: even as freedom drew closer for her, she worried more and more about her family in Warsaw.

Natek was at his wit's end. He thought that fresh air would do her good and offered her his hand to lead her up to the deck. She took it, tried to stand, and collapsed. He could only watch helplessly as tears flowed down her cheeks.

≋ For months after my husband and I separated, I lay on my couch, nursing the ache in my heart. When a friend told me that she had been at the hospital to see a woman who was hours away from dying of cancer, I didn't feel sad, but envious. I imagined lying in that hospital bed surrounded by love, peacefully drifting into an endless sleep.

My brother Bob was a champion during this time. He's a doctor with a busy family practice, but I'd phone him at work as well as at home when I felt like I couldn't take any more, and he would let me talk. He said he didn't see the separation coming either, which made me feel less crazy. But mostly he just let me talk.

Shades of Green

AS THE SHIP NEARED the Japanese port of Tsuruga, Zosia's stomach was calmed by the tranquility of the city's protected harbour. Beautiful Wakasa Bay lay beneath snow-capped mountains and, from a distance, the buildings on shore looked like dollhouses to Zosia. Once the boat had docked, the houses didn't look much bigger; they were so delicate that she was convinced they were made out of cardboard.

Zosia and Natek's nerves were still jangled, though. All the way from Vladivostok, they had agonized over how they would be able to communicate with Japanese immigration officials. How would they be able to explain not having a Curaçao visa? What if they were turned away at the border? Would they have to sail back to Russia, and live out their lives in Siberia?

As Zosia and Natek disembarked, they and the other Jewish refugees were greeted by a Caucasian man who introduced himself as a representative of the Joint Distribution Committee (JDC); the New York–based relief agency had lived up to its commitments to Consul Sugihara, and funds for housing, food, and other services were already in place. He spoke to the Japanese immigration official on their behalf and assisted Natek and Zosia as they presented their documentation. The Japanese official asked them a few terse questions, then quickly stamped their passport. It was so quick that Zosia and Natek stood waiting for a second round of questioning, not realizing that they had completed the admission process. The JDC representative had to tell them that they were free to go.

Once all of the refugees had passed through immigration, the same official walked them to the station so that they could catch a train to Kobe, where they would be housed. Everything Zosia saw on that walk was completely different from anything she had seen in Europe. The buses streaming down the streets of Tsuruga were cleaner and sleeker. She herself felt filthy and unkempt next to the Japanese people, many of whom wore nose masks to protect themselves from germs. The women walked along the streets in elaborately embroidered silk kimonos that danced in the light. Zosia wondered what life was like for these women and whether they were as happy as their clothes made them seem.

Once they were on the train travelling through the countryside, everything was green, magnificently green, in a multitude of shades: golden-green, blue-green, grey-green, even a green that was almost red. Through her window, Zosia watched agricultural labourers in boat-shaped hats wade knee-deep through wet fields to pull up straw-like plants. Other workers bundled the plants into long narrow sheaves, then tied the sheaves to bamboo fences to dry. Natek explained that they were harvesting rice.

When they arrived in Kobe, the refugees boarded another bus, which took them to a neighbourhood of small two-storey buildings. There, each refugee was assigned to a house, or *heime* as they were called in Yiddish. Zosia and Natek carried their luggage up to the second floor of their *heime* and put it down in one of the three rooms. The room was clean and better equipped than any they had seen since Warsaw. Moreover, it was free. This was a great relief to Natek, who was always worried about running out of money.

They introduced themselves to the others who shared the room and were happy to learn that they all spoke Polish. "Where can I send a telegram?" Natek asked. A tall, dark-haired man gave him directions, and Natek left to cable his mother that they had arrived safely.

The refugees weren't allowed to work, and sometimes when the weather was warm, a group of them would spend the afternoon in one of Kobe's many parks. These were highly manicured gardens and, from almost anywhere, one could hear the soothing sound of a stream trickling into a tranquil pond.

On one such trip, a group of white-robed monks with shaved heads meditated near the foreigners. Zosia sat silently, forced into contemplation by the presence of the pious men, and drifted back to Poland — not the war years, but her early years, when she played with her friends in Saski Park then, exhausted by all of her running around, relaxed with Panna Pola under a giant evergreen, her head cushioned by Panna's soft leg. Then the monks began to chant and Zosia's eyes focused on the giant statue of Buddha in front of her.

In 1941, Japan was at war with China but had not yet joined the conflict between Germany and the Allies, and there were no obvious food shortages in Japan. At the large open-air market in Kobe, all sorts of exotic fruits and vegetables were for sale — raw, cooked, however you liked them — as well as meat and fresh fish.

Zosia and Natek purchased dried sausage, sugar, tea and coffee, which they parcelled up and sent to their families.

They were not sure if the food they were sending was arriving at its destination. For weeks after they arrived in Japan, neither Zosia nor Natek heard from their family members in Poland. But letters did arrive eventually. The first was from Natek's mother. It was dated February 5, 1941, and assured them that their parcels were getting through. This was good news, of course, but the note contained no information of any sort about the ghetto.

Like all of the Jewish refugees in Kobe, Zosia and Natek worried constantly about the families they'd left behind. Were conditions crowded in the ghetto? Were family members suffering? Were all of them still alive? No one wanted to believe the worst, so they consoled themselves that conditions, though hard, were probably bearable.

Lolek and Danka arrived in Kobe six weeks after Natek and Zosia. At first, the brothers were happy to be reunited, but that joy was short-lived. Lolek was not interested in sharing a room in a *heime*. Natek tried to convince him to save the substantial sum of money he'd set aside in New York, but Lolek paid him no heed. Like the other wealthy Jews, he rented his own quarters and resumed his lavish parties, to which Natek was rarely invited.

As winter moved into spring, Zosia and Natek discovered that, somehow, mail flowed more freely between Poland and Japan than it had between Poland and Lithuania. In June, Natek was overjoyed to receive another letter from his mother.

"I thank Natek for the parcel of tea and sausage, which I can always use," she began. "Thanks to God all of us are feeling well but the lack of news from Father worries me very much. I got a card from Lolek from Tokyo. Please write more often since this is my only pleasure."

Natek was troubled by his mother's reference to his father. Szaja had not been heard from since he disappeared on the road home to Warsaw from Lvov in Eastern Poland almost a year and a half earlier. It was obvious that his father was not coming back and Natek was haunted by what might have happened to him. Still, what could he say to his mother if she was determined to keep hope alive?

One morning, Natek awoke with his face as white as chalk and his whole body in uncontrollable spasms. Zosia felt his forehead; it was burning up. "You've got to go to a doctor," she said. "We'll try the hospital down the street."

"Your husband has Manju fever," a Polish-speaking doctor named Hudechuk told Zosia. "It is a serious illness, an infectious disease. He must be immediately admitted and kept in isolation. You cannot visit him as long as he is contagious."

Natek's room was on the ground floor, with one window looking onto the street. If Zosia stood on tiptoe, she could just make him out. But that was uncomfortable; she needed something to stand on. The hospital staff gave her a sturdy box and, climbing onto it, she was able to peer through the window and see him lying in his bed. From then on, she stood on the box every day.

After three long weeks, Natek was released from the hospital. Although no longer contagious, he was extremely thin and weak. Zosia, who always felt so protected by Natek, now took care of him — in a small room shared with seven other people. Lolek and Danka, who had their own house, never invited Natek and Zosia to share the comfort of their home.

Natek's illness made Zosia feel so vulnerable that she wrote to her parents and siblings often during those panicky weeks, although she began to wonder if she would ever see them again.

Once Natek recovered, he was determined to travel to America as soon as possible. Japan had not yet declared war against the Allies, but the mounting political tension bothered him. "Germany and Japan are too friendly," he told Zosia. "How can we be sure that they will continue to treat us well? If the Americans enter the war, they will do so on the side of the Allies, and we'll be trapped here!"

So, just as he had journeyed frequently from Vilnius to Kaunas in Lithuania, Natek trekked to Tokyo on a regular basis to explore every possible route out of the country. At the American embassy, he was told that his expired visa could not be extended. Uncertain of getting a new visa to the US, he also inquired at the Australian and Canadian embassies. And he kept in regular touch with the Polish embassy because countries such as the United States would sometimes allocate a certain number of visas to other nations.

One day in the middle of June 1941, while navigating through the crowds on a narrow Tokyo street, Natek was startled to hear someone call his name. He turned, and there was Professor Szpilfogel waving to him.

"Natek, how good to see you! So you're in Japan too. Who would have thought it?"

The two men shook hands warmly.

"It is always such a pleasure to see you, Professor," Natek said. "How fate draws us together!" He wanted to hug his old professor but propriety prevailed.

"Did you enjoy working on the kibbutz?" Szpilfogel asked.

"Very much. I was fortunate that you told me about that job."

"Where are you going from here?"

"I want to go to New York. I had hoped that the Americans would extend my old visa, but they won't, so I'm on a waiting list. I've been going there at least once a week, but so far I have no reason to believe I'll receive one any time soon."

"Would you be interested in going to Canada?" the professor asked.

"Certainly!"

"It is my understanding that the Canadian government has given the Poles some visas for professionals with your qualifications. You'd be wise to go to the Polish embassy immediately. I believe a ship is leaving for Canada quite soon. Tell them that I advised you of the opportunity."

Natek thanked Professor Szpilfogel with an enthusiastic handshake. He went directly to the Polish embassy and was met by a tall, balding man with a pallid face. Since Natek had been to see the same official only two days before, the man gave him an exasperated look.

"Nothing new to tell you," he said, and turned away.

"I have just spoken to Professor Szpilfogel of the Agricultural University of Warsaw," Natek explained. "I was a student of his. He told me that the Canadians have given this embassy visas for professionals with my qualifications. My wife and I would like to go to Canada."

The man looked dubious. He rummaged through a mass of papers and shook his head. Then he opened a desk drawer and pulled out a file.

"Ah yes. We do have such a visa available. Do you have proof of your qualifications?"

Natek handed him the certificates that he always brought to Tokyo.

"Everything seems in order," the man said. "You are welcome to the visa, but you do know that there is only one. I am afraid that your wife will not be able to go with you."

Natek felt as though his heart had stopped.

"I cannot go without my wife," he said.

"I am sorry, but that's the way it is."

Natek did not know what to say. How could they refuse to give Zosia a visa?

"Please, sir, could I have a day to think about it?"

"I understand how you feel," the man replied, suddenly sounding sympathetic, "but there is little I can do. Still, if you want to take a day to think about it, that's fine."

Natek took a bus to the station and boarded the next train to Kobe. At home, he excitedly told Zosia the good and bad news. "Of course I won't go to Canada without you," he assured her, "but come with me to Tokyo! You know that I have better luck when you are with me. If they see you, we will have a better chance of convincing them to give you a visa."

The next morning, they caught the first train for Tokyo and went straight to the Polish embassy. The same man was behind the desk, leafing through what looked like the same stack of papers. Natek introduced Zosia.

"Sir, my wife wants me to take the visa, but I cannot. If I left without her she would be all alone, because all of her family is in Warsaw. Who knows how long it would take for her join me in Canada? Zosia wants to go to Canada as much as I do, so perhaps if you ask the Canadians they will be compassionate and give you another visa."

"I'm sorry," the official said. "I sympathize with your situation, but there is only one visa."

The man avoided looking at Zosia. She could tell that he felt terrible.

"Please," Natek said, "I cannot leave my wife. Please try to do something."

Zosia watched with her sad blue eyes. The man finally looked up at her.

"Come back in a few hours," he said, "and I will see what I can do."

So Natek and Zosia walked around Tokyo. Natek suggested

that they go to a park to relax, and they found a small garden. They sat under a large cherry tree. The blossoms were gone and the branches were covered with vibrant green growth. They sat in its shadow saying nothing, just holding hands.

When they returned to the Polish embassy, the man smiled as they walked in the door.

"We have found another visa! Your wife can go with you, but you must go to the Canadian embassy right now. A ship is leaving right away."

"From Canada we will go to the United States!" Natek exclaimed. "We're going to America!"

Natek and Zosia kissed and kissed, oblivious to the blushing official staring at them from behind the counter. They thanked him profusely and hurried off to the Canadian embassy. As they walked, Zosia could not take her eyes off her husband. Where would she be without him?

The Canadian embassy required a $4,000 guarantee, which threw them into a panic for a day, but Natek contacted Mr. Catz, who put up the money. Finally, a weary-looking blond official at the Canadian embassy stamped the passport that Natek and Zosia shared: "Non-immigrant. Admitted for the duration of the war only."

"You understand, you can only stay in Canada until the war is over," he explained slowly. "Then you must go back to Poland."

"We understand," said Natek.

The man seemed satisfied that he'd made his point, and handed back the passport. Then he told them that they should not waste any time before buying tickets because a ship was leaving for Vancouver very soon.

"Where is Vancouver?" Natek asked.

"On the Pacific Ocean, north of California. You will not be far from the American border."

"Is it a big city?"

"In Canada it is."

"Is it far from Toronto or Montreal?" Natek asked, naming the only Canadian cities that he had ever heard of.

"Very far."

Natek translated this for Zosia. Then he reassured her, "As soon as we find jobs and earn some money, we will go to Toronto or Montreal. Perhaps we'll obtain visas to the United States and go to New York."

The next day, June 26, 1941, the young couple boarded the *Hie Maru*, an aging freighter in the Yokohama harbour. They carried their few belongings and two American $20 bills, which was all the money they had.

They were bound for Vancouver.

Natek and Zosia with a group of Jewish refugees,
Kobe, Japan 1941. Natek is second from left in the back row;
Zosia is fourth from left near the back.

Natek with a group of Jewish refugees in Kobe, Japan, 25 May 1941.
Natek is second on the left.

Zosia and Natek along with other Jewish refugees on board the Japanese
ship *Hie Maru* on their way from Japan to Vancouver, June 1941.
Zosia is third from left, back row. Natek is below her and to the right.

Zosia and Natek out for a stroll together soon after
they arrived in Vancouver

Zosia with her son George, Burnaby, September 1944

Natek with his son George on his shoulders, 1944

Zosia would take her son George in the stroller with
her when she went to work, Vancouver, 1944.

Natek with other Canadian soldiers in training at Prince Rupert, 1944

Zosia on the front porch of their Burnaby home, c. 1951

Zosia and Natek in Vancouver, shortly before Natek's death in 1986

The author Barbara Ruth Bluman with her brother Bob in
Cabo San Lucas, 2001, not long before Barbara's death from cancer

Zosia and her family, September 2000. Zosia is front centre with
daughter Barbara and son George on her right, and son Bob on
her left, with granddaughter Danielle on the far right
(back row) with her brothers, Sam and Mike next to her.

I I

Swamper

≈ I have often jogged along Spanish Banks, one of the beaches that line the harbour my parents sailed into, and I regularly marvel at life's ability to reinvent itself.

In February of 1999, just over two years after Drew left, I was jogging along this beach with my good friend Gail when we ran into her ex-partner, Jim. He invited us both to his fiftieth birthday party and I went, although Gail declined.

Jim and I talked at the party, and a few days later, he phoned and asked if I'd like to attend a basketball game with him. I said that I'd love to, except that I hate basketball! We decided to go to dinner instead. Over the next few weeks, we fell into the habit of going to restaurants and being the last customers to leave. This wasn't about romance: we would just yak for hours, Jim talking about his life, and me talking about mine. It was luxurious to be able to speak so openly to a man — one who wasn't my brother!

At the end of our evenings, we'd usually have a pleasant and polite goodnight, but one evening, after we'd had a few drinks with friends of Jim's, all of a sudden we were embracing like two enthusiastic teenagers on my front porch! Something deep inside of me began to relax. It was as if I could feel the blood returning to my limbs for the first time since Drew left. ❧

When the *Hie Maru* docked in Vancouver on July 9, 1941, Zosia barely registered the beach; to her, the city appeared to be wedged between the ocean and the steep mountains.

Every sort of contradictory emotion flooded her mind as she disembarked. On the one hand, she felt confident that she and Natek would find jobs to support themselves while they waited out the war in this strange place. But then she thought of the subtly desperate tone of her family's letters and of the increasing reports of suffering in the ghetto.

The passengers were escorted to the Canadian immigration office. Natek told the officer that he and his wife intended to return to Poland once the war was over, but the officer wanted further assurance that they did not intend to remain permanently in Canada.

"Our families and our business are in Warsaw," Natek said. "We have to go back."

This satisfied the immigration officer. He told them that they could proceed.

With the other Jewish refugees — fourteen had cleared immigration — they were driven to the Jewish Community Centre at Oak Street and Eleventh Avenue, where they were introduced to a couple who invited them to stay in their home in the Kitsilano neighbourhood. Zosia and Natek were overwhelmed by this kindness.

After two days in which Natek had been unable to find work, however, their hosts made it clear that they were no longer welcome. Zosia could not help thinking that, on the day of their arrival, these people had only been showing off in front of their friends.

She and Natek were not familiar with the city and had no idea where to begin, but they eventually found a small housekeeping room at 1173 Nelson Street, which rented for $3.50 per week. It was in a poor section of the downtown area and was only a small room with a bed against the wall, a hotplate, a few utensils, and a bathroom down the hall, but they were relieved to have their own place.

Still, they had to find employment. Over the next few weeks, they were invited to the homes of several well-to-do Jewish families. Their hosts showed them their large, well-appointed houses, and inevitably asked what they could do to help them. "Do you know of any jobs for me?" Natek would ask. The response was always silence.

As the weeks passed, Natek became increasingly anxious. They were down to their last $20 bill and, although he had no job prospects, he was too proud to tap into the money put up by Mr. Catz. Then, through connections made by Benton Brown, the honorary Polish consul in Vancouver, Natek was offered an interview with Jack Diamond, who ran a packing house.

When Natek went to see Mr. Diamond, he was hired immediately as a swamper. He didn't know what that was, but Mr. Diamond knew that Natek had a degree in agricultural engineering so Natek was confident that his position would reflect his university education. When he returned home to Zosia that evening he was happier than he'd been in weeks.

However, when Natek reported for work the next day, he

learned that the swamping job consisted of delivering sides of beef to grocery stores. In Poland, this was considered one of the lowest forms of employment. Natek was devastated, but he needed the job and persevered. Unused to heavy physical labour, he found that many evenings he was too sore to move. Zosia rubbed liniment into his back every night. Natek's only comfort was that now he could release the money Mr. Catz had put up so that it would be available to Danka and Lolek.

Zosia also looked for work, but with no skills and less English than her husband, her prospects were dim. At first, she could only find piecework as a sewer, but she enrolled in a night-school course to improve her English, and it was not long before she spoke well enough to be hired as a salesgirl in a store at Main and Water streets, selling workmen's clothing.

Natek took an evening class in metal lathing, hoping that it would help him find work in the war industry. Sure enough, after completing the course, he was hired by Boeing to work in a shipyard. He quit being a swamper.

A few months passed before Natek or Zosia received any letters from home. Then, on August 10, 1941, Zosia's mother Estera wrote, "You don't need to worry about us. Somehow together we are getting along just fine and we are waiting for the moment when we will see you again."

Zosia and Natek wanted to believe Estera's assurances that the family was fine and that they need not worry, but all the news stories told them the opposite. Apparently, German and Austrian Jews were being deported to Polish ghettos. There were reports, too, of torture and killing. They hoped that this was just war propaganda but, having lived under German occupation, Zosia feared that the stories were true.

Lolek and Danka had not been able to obtain visas to the United States, so they had accepted visas to Australia. Lolek wrote that he would try to get to New York once the war was over.

About a month after receiving Estera's letters, Zosia and Natek received a letter from Gina's husband, Jurek. "We are so happy to know that, by some lucky fate, you have managed to arrive in such a peaceful place," he wrote on September 21, 1941. "Let's hope that our wishes will come true in the very near future." Zosia struggled to comprehend the letter; Jurek and Gina were obviously not in a peaceful place.

With family in Europe, Natek and Zosia took the war news personally. They cried with each German victory. And, when the Japanese bombed Pearl Harbor on December 7, 1941, and the Americans entered the war on the side of the Allies, they rejoiced. "We will win the war now," Natek said. "The Americans will do it!" Over the course of the day, they laughed and cried and made all sorts of plans about what they would do when they saw their families again.

After Jurek's letter, however, the correspondence stopped.

About six months after Jim and I became involved, I was lying in bed with him when I felt the lump in my breast. My breast cancer diagnosis was followed by surgery in June of 1999, then chemotherapy as well as radiation that lasted until November. I felt great for a while, but in March of 2000, a diagnosis of colorectal cancer explained my creeping fatigue.

Treating my colon cancer was a huge time commitment. I endured endless rounds of blood tests, medical consultations and CAT scans, as well as more chemotherapy and radiation. I felt like I was falling again — but this time I allowed myself to be caught.

Jim showered me with attention. In many long conversations with my brothers George and Bob, we brought our childhoods back to life, the pain as well as the pleasure. I felt so grateful to have such loving siblings. I spent hour after precious hour conversing with my children and, as our trust in each other grew, we exchanged increasingly intimate confidences.

On June 28, 2000, I underwent extensive surgery: my rectum was removed along with my primary tumour, and two malignant lymph nodes in my groin were excised. A colostomy bag was attached, which required my being stitched both front and back so that I was only comfortable lying on my side.

It was summer, so as soon as I was able to leave the hospital I went to the beach house. Lying on the living room sofa, I could see and hear the waves. Despite some pain, I felt at peace, and the post-surgery news was encouraging: the doctors reported that my tumour had shrunk under the combined onslaught of radiation and chemo, and they were optimistic about my chances.

Weeks later, I was stronger and went for short walks along the roller-coaster road that cuts a swath from the beach house through the dense evergreens of the mountain's temperate rainforest. In my first efforts, I felt weak and took each step as carefully as if I were walking a tightrope. By the end of the summer, I felt stronger and could walk up to twelve kilometres along the mountain road.

Jim said that I looked more beautiful than ever. I wore little make-up and everyone agreed that the short hairstyle I had favoured since my breast cancer treatment was flattering. All I know is that I felt loved. It was amazing to me how much richer my relationships had grown since my marriage dissolved.

Three months post-surgery, I felt as energetic as ever. But something was not right. I felt discomfort whenever I stood or walked. As days passed, walking became more and more painful until it was unbearable.

My oncologist, Dr. Barbara Melosky, examined me and found a very small node in the anal area. I was admitted to the Cancer

Agency and, over the course of a week, more tests were done. With moist eyes, Dr. Melosky gave me the worst possible news: my colon cancer had recurred and metastasized. "It doesn't make sense," she told me. "You look too good!"

But the scans made it clear. There was a large tumour on my liver and there were four smaller ones on my lungs. My prognosis was grim: a full cure was no longer possible. The cancer was progressing rapidly, and Dr. Melosky estimated I had three months to live unless an effective chemotherapy treatment could be found to put me into remission.

On the advice of Dr. Karen Gelmon, another oncologist at the Cancer Agency, I travelled to the Mayo Clinic in Rochester, Minnesota, for a second opinion. My brother Bob and my oldest son Michael came with me. The pain in my buttocks was so unbearable that I reluctantly agreed to be taken in a wheelchair. Looking healthy, despite my galloping disease, and dressed elegantly, I felt like a fraud. Some people looked at me suspiciously, others with pity. I'm not sure which was worse.

My daughter Danielle, twenty years old at the time, was in New Zealand when I learned that the cancer had recurred. She had been away three weeks and was about to fly to Bali when she checked her email and learned the news. She called home sobbing uncontrollably, and insisted on returning to Vancouver immediately.

Even my mother lost her composure and broke down in my presence.

It is difficult, and for some of us, impossible, to imagine that we are dying, even when death hovers in the shadows, be it tumours running amok in your body or Nazi goosesteps behind you. ❧

12

A Birth and a Letter

ZOSIA BECAME PREGNANT in the fall of 1942. The pregnancy had not been planned and Natek wasn't pleased; he always worried about money and felt that they were not yet in a position to support a child. "We should get established first," he pleaded with Zosia. But Zosia was already overflowing with love for the little embryo within her and would not be dissuaded.

Natek had plans of his own. His job with Boeing was essential to the war effort, and all those working in such positions were exempt from military service. But Natek did not care. "I have decided to enlist in the Canadian army," he told Zosia. "I will never forgive myself if I don't fight against the Nazis."

Zosia didn't want him to go, but she didn't try to dissuade him either; he had made up his mind. Still, she worried because, if

Natek died overseas, she would be all alone with the baby. The prospect was too horrible to think about. "Take it one day at a time," she told herself.

Natek went to the recruitment office to enlist, but heard nothing afterwards. He made inquiries. "You are not a British subject," he was told, "so you cannot swear allegiance to the King." Zosia was relieved.

On June 3, 1943, she gave birth to a son. Despite his initial reservations, Natek was overjoyed to hold the child in his arms. He still had one of the two $20 bills they had brought from Japan. "I will never part with that money now," he told Zosia. "Our son shall have it."

It had been more than a year since Zosia and Natek had heard from their families. And now there were reports of mass exterminations of Polish Jews. It was possible that their families were no longer alive. Natek and Zosia didn't want to believe this but, if it were true, they would have no reason to return to Poland.

In this context, naming the baby was not an easy task. Their son had been born in Canada and was a Canadian citizen, so they decided that he should have a Canadian name. They decided on George, because no name could be "sounder" than that of the King of England.

Natek continued his efforts to enlist in the army, explaining that he was a Jew and had a moral obligation to fight the Germans. Eventually he was accepted. On June 26, 1944, Natek entered the Canadian Army and, not long afterwards, he was sent to Prince Rupert, a Pacific port hundreds of miles north of Vancouver.

Zosia and Natek had moved a number of times, most recently because a neighbour had complained about George's crying. When he went north, Natek left Zosia in an apartment that was located in a seedy part of downtown. There were bootleggers up and down their block, and directly across the street was the Penthouse, a notorious nightclub that openly advertised its X-rated shows and, less openly, provided a range of sexual services. With Natek gone, Zosia was afraid to go out alone in the evening. She worried that men would accost her. Sometimes, drunks would bang on her door and Zosia would sit petrified.

Natek was home on leave from Prince Rupert when Victory Day was declared in Europe on May 8, 1945. From their apartment, they could hear people rejoicing and screaming in the street below as crowds streamed into the downtown core. They took Georgie, who was not quite two, by the hand and went out to join the feverish party. Both Natek and Zosia were crying.

In the days that followed, they began their search to find their relatives. They registered their names with the Jewish organizations involved in the relief efforts, hoping that family members might make contact with them through that route, and pored over the organizations' registers for a familiar name. They wrote to Mr. Catz, asking whether family members had written care of him, and he wrote back that he had heard nothing. Lolek had no better luck in making inquiries from Australia.

Weeks passed, then months, and still they heard nothing. Thanks to the newspapers, the extent of the Holocaust had become common knowledge — an unfathomable number, as many as six million, had been killed — but Zosia and Natek refused to give up hope.

Natek was discharged from the army on April 30, 1946, and decided to return to university. Because he was a veteran, his tuition was paid for, along with minimal living expenses. He and Zosia no longer talked about returning to Warsaw. Still, they refused to give up the dream that one day they would be reunited with their families. After all, Europe was in chaos and communication was difficult —' more difficult for them because Poland and Vancouver were on opposite sides of the world.

By the spring of 1947, Natek was enrolled in university, and Zosia was working as a saleslady on Saturdays, when Natek stayed home to look after Georgie. One Saturday in May, the sky was blue, blossoms were bursting forth everywhere and the mountains were still speckled with snow. As the store was closing, Natek walked in with their three-year-old son.

"We've come to pick you up," he told Zosia.

Georgie and his mother cuddled and played all the way home. It was not until they were back in the apartment that Zosia realized how morose Natek was; he had not said anything the entire way home. As she took off her coat, he handed her a letter. It was from Palestine.

"It's from Olga," he said.

Zosia stared at the letter in her hands. Olga. Heniek's wife. Why hadn't Heniek himself written? Georgie wanted to play with her, and it was with some difficulty that Natek extricated the child from his mother and took him outside. Zosia was left alone to read.

Tel Aviv

March 24, 1947

Dearest Zosia,

It is hard to describe how I am feeling as I write this letter. The people dearest to me live again, and it fills my eyes with tears and my heart with pain to know that I am the only one who survived while they all perished. There is no trace left of the Hoffenberg family. It's as if they never existed.

I shall describe to you as accurately as I can what it was like.

Three months after your escape to Vilnius, Heniek and I returned to Warsaw. The establishment of the Ghetto was already under-way, so Heniek and I moved to my apartment block on Slishka

Street, which was located within the Ghetto borders. Your father and mother moved in with Ruta, Julek, and their daughter Hanusia to Panska Street since, as you know, Ruta and Julek owned an apartment block there and it was also located in the Ghetto area.

We all lived in the Ghetto for two years. Of course, life was very, very difficult. Nobody could make any money and we were selling things from home.

In February 1942, your father got very sick with typhoid fever. There was an epidemic of typhoid in the Ghetto. Your father was sick for sixteen days. Every day, three doctors [from inside the Ghetto] came to see him and two nurses looked after him — one for the day shift and one for the night. His diabetes made the cure very difficult. Three days after becoming sick, he went into a coma. He called for you often.

Of course, Heniek and I were there every day and night. Because I know something about nursing, I helped to give him injections and nursed him. Even a king couldn't have had better care than he had but, unfortunately, no human effort could save him. Within three days of his falling ill, terrible complications occurred: brain infection and pneumonia. Your father suffered terribly. He was in pain and cried constantly. Sixteen days later, he died without having regained consciousness.

We put up a beautiful monument. Later, we found out that he was actually luckier than those who were burned or buried half alive in Treblinka; he died in his own bed, surrounded by his loving family. We surrounded your mother with lots of love and care so she wouldn't feel so lonely.

Your cousin Salek's mother was taken as a hostage by the Gestapo and she never returned.

Transfer of people to camps in unbelievable numbers started in July 1942. This lasted three and a half months and, during this period, 12,000 people were sent to Treblinka daily. I lost my mother when she was sent. They snatched Gina's husband Jurek from the street when he went out to save his sister Marysia. They also captured your sister Gina and her little boy Grzesio.

For three months, we had to hide in the bunkers, cellars and attics so that we would not be caught and sent away. The houses were surrounded. All of the Jews had to work in factories for the Germans, but even these places of work were not safe.

It was also during that action that your Aunt Hinda, the one with the retarded son, was killed on the street by the Germans after they undressed her completely and robbed her of a lot of gold, diamonds and dollars.

Half a million were sent away to Treblinka. After this action, very few Jews remained in the Ghetto.

At the beginning of 1943, we thought that the remaining Jews would survive, since the Germans needed us for work. Everyone had an *Ausweis*, a paper that gave them the right to work and, at the same time, the right to live. But, when the Germans started another action and a blockade, we knew that it was the end.

There were three possibilities of survival: to escape to the Aryan side, to spend the rest of the war in a bunker, or to be transferred to Poniatowa, a labour camp in which all the Jews from the Ghetto were to be settled. The Ghetto was to be completely liquidated by May. Ruta's husband Julek was interested in moving to the Aryan side, but I think that he didn't want to pay as much money as they demanded from him for hiding four people — Julek, Ruta, their little girl Hanusia and your mother — so he decided that, when the time came, he would let them be taken to Poniatowa.

I decided to go to the Aryan side and I begged everyone to do the same, but without success. Because Heniek was a manager in a factory, he wasn't too anxious to leave. Just the same, though, he found a place for us on the Aryan side and we moved all of our belongings to it. I moved there. Heniek and I had obtained false Aryan papers and I was walking around as an Aryan. I started looking for a place for your mother, Ruta, Julek, and their daughter Hanusia. I found a place for them and I intended to force them all to come.

At four o'clock in the afternoon on the first day of Passover, I was supposed to get a phone call from Heniek about moving the whole family to the Aryan side. But, at twelve noon, the Ghetto uprising started. The Ghetto was immediately surrounded by the army, police, tanks, and planes dropping bombs. I was living on Senatorska Street, next to the Ghetto and, for the next three weeks, I watched the Ghetto burn right in front of my eyes. Every house was bombed. The sky was black from the smoke. Mothers and children jumped out of windows from three floors up and higher, knowing what fate awaited them. Over the loudspeakers, the Germans announced that whoever surrendered of their own free will would be transported to Poniatowa. I found out later that that was where the rest of the family Hoffenberg, including Heniek, went.

After this, I suffered from a terrible depression. I was lying down all day and I didn't want to eat. My brother Joziek and his wife Hala, who were hiding on the Aryan side, thought that this was my end. They forced me to work in order to get me out of this state of mind. I worked like a horse in an Aryan household, looking after two children from five a.m. to ten p.m.

Three months later, I received a card from Heniek from Poniatowa: "SAVE ME! Send me some papers and money!" That same day, I sold the diamonds and sent him money and Aryan papers.

A special woman was going to bring him over. In two days, I got a receipt saying that he received the papers and money, and that, within the next three days, he would be with me. He never came. On the way, the Germans shot him. This is all. . . . In six weeks, every person in Poniatowa was murdered. No survivors.

That summer, I went with the Aryan people I worked for to Boenerowo, a little town outside Warsaw, where I stayed until the end of the war. Joziek and Hala soon came to Boenerowo too, but they were denounced and taken to the Gestapo, where they were going to be shot. They undressed Joziek completely and saw that he was a Jew but, by some miracle, they let him and Hala go free. I found them a room in Boenerowo, and thus we survived the war. It was unbelievably difficult to have to pretend to be Christian and play that role.

I have described to you everything briefly, just to give you an idea of how it was. After the war, we left Poland and, through the help of a Zionist organization, we went illegally to Palestine. On the way, I stayed six months in Austria and six months in Italy. All of that time I looked for you. I sent announcements to American newspapers, without getting any results. Finally, my brother found you.

Zosia, I need 100 pounds to buy a room. Right now I pay eight pounds a month rent and I work as a nurse in a hospital making eighteen pounds a month. It is very hard over here. My brother is not well. Here, doctors don't make very much money. He gets twenty-five pounds a month. I would greatly appreciate your help.

Best regards and kisses to Natek.

Love,
Olga

Zosia put down the letter. She cried and cried, but the tears gave her no comfort. Natek and Georgie came home, and Georgie crawled over to his mother. Zosia picked him up and wiped away her tears. She had no choice but to carry on with her life.

13

My Jewish Body

I want to carry on with my life. Jim and I search the Internet for new chemotherapy trials — often late into the night — and, if one looks promising, we send the information over to Bob for his opinion. I try anything that sounds worthwhile, which means that I have tried a lot. In February, Bob took me to Cabo San Lucas in between rounds of chemotherapy. Jim and I have taken trips to New York and London.

As my body struggles to stay alive, I am aware that I am Jewish on a deep physical level.

I had little contact with the Jewish religion as I grew up. Like many Holocaust survivors, my father blamed organized religion for the world's woes. My parents were not affiliated with any synagogue, and while they often attended services on High Holidays,

*Barbara (second from the left) with her newly discovered extended
Hoffenberg family — Eva, Esther, Adele, Salek and Theo — Paris, 1969*

they would never take my brothers or me with them. I did not
enter a synagogue until I was an adult.

Still, I have always felt my ethnicity as though it were part of my
limbs and torso, my hands, feet and head. I know that the members of my family are like fresh shoots poking through the soil
where there was once a proud old tree.

Thinking of our family members, I recall how, years ago, on January 27, 1968, my mother's eyes were drawn to a tiny newspaper
article about a South African physician named Raymond Hoffenberg who had played a vital part in Dr. Christiaan Barnard's first
heart transplant surgery in 1967.

Hoffenberg is not a common surname, and my mother wondered
if Raymond could be her cousin Jasiek who had trained as a physician in Italy prior to World War II. Many Jews who emigrated to

English-speaking countries after the war had anglicized their names. So she wrote to Dr. Hoffenberg care of the British Medical Research Council, and asked him if they might be related.

Dr. Hoffenberg wrote back that he was not Jasiek Hoffenberg but a native-born South African whose family had emigrated from Poland in the 1880s, and if he was related to my mother he thought it was a distant relationship at best. However, he informed her that he had just received a similar letter from a Sam Hoffenberg who lived in Paris, and included his address.

My mother wrote to Sam immediately.

I was eighteen years old, at home by myself, when the letter from Salek Hoffenberg came through our mail slot. I was so excited that I tore the letter open, but of course it was written in Polish. I couldn't wait for my parents to come home from work, so I rushed to the home of their Polish friends and asked them to translate for me.

I learned that my Uncle Salek — or Sam — had four children, including a daughter, Esther, who was my age. I cried with happiness. I cried with relief.

I saved the money from my weekend job and twelve months later, after my first year of university, I flew to Paris. At the airport, Esther and I rushed into each other's arms, never doubting that we were cousins though we had never seen a photo of the other. Symcha Hoffenberg was my grandfather and Esther's great uncle, and we both had his clear blue eyes. ✎

First Generation Afterword

Zosia Hoffenberg Bluman

THIS BOOK IS A project Barbie started a few years before her heroic fight with cancer. Barbie interviewed me for months and months, trying to get a total picture of my life — her mother's life — in pre-war Warsaw and the years afterwards. (Unfortunately my dear Nathan had passed away in April 1986.) My life fascinated Barbie, a life that was so different from hers. I was delighted to be able to confide in her my memories, both pleasant and not so pleasant. I was amazed and flattered that my Barbie, who I admired so much, my busy lawyer-arbitrator daughter who was in the midst of bringing up three wonderful children, and who contributed her time and knowledge to many worthy causes, would also find time to record my life.

Even now, it is hard for me to comprehend that I, the youngest in my family, with the fewest life experiences, was the only one to have survived. This was largely thanks to Nathan's foresight and determination.

This book is Barbie's gift to me as well as to her children, Michael, Danielle and Sam, and to her brothers and nephews. I hope it will help to perpetuate the memory of our lost families.

Thank you, Barbie, for documenting my life. We love you so much.

Barbie passed away on September 8, 2001. Her spirit and soul are with us forever.

Third Generation Afterword

Danielle Bluman Low (Schroeder)

I STARE CONFIDENTLY at my reflection in the mirror, but it is not my own eyes that I am focusing on; it's the brilliance of the blue necklace. It hangs around my neck as a precious symbol of my mother's unforgettable blue eyes.

As the only third-generation woman in our family, it falls to me to conclude this manuscript, to add my voice to my mother's and my grandmother's as I consider their extraordinary legacies and how they have shaped my life.

First, I want to honour Chiune Sugihara, the extraordinary Japanese diplomat who made it possible for my grandparents to escape from Europe and the Holocaust.

Most estimates put the number of lives he saved at between 6,000 and 10,000. Having decided to defy his superiors in the diplomatic service, he reportedly worked for between eighteen and twenty hours every day from July 31 to September 4, 1940. Eyewitnesses said that, even as his train pulled away from the station in Kaunas, he continued to throw visas out the window to people in the crowd.

Sugihara was serving in Bucharest, Romania, when Soviet troops marched into that country at the end of the war. The Soviets imprisoned him and his family in a POW camp for eighteen months before returning them to Japan. In 1947, the Japanese government asked their former star diplomat to resign from the diplomatic service. He was forced to look for part-time work and eventually became a manager for an export company.

In 1985, the government of Israel named Chiune Sugihara one of the Righteous among Nations. Because he was too ill to travel to Israel, his wife Yukiko and son Hiroki attended the ceremony in his stead.

When he was asked why he risked so much to follow his moral principles, he quoted an old Samurai saying: "Even a hunter cannot kill a bird that flies to him for refuge."

I also want to honour the tenacity that my mother and grandmother shared — and which shaped their lives in so many different and complicated ways.

On October 15, 2004, my grandma died of colon cancer.

She spent the last month and a half of her life at the Palliative Care Unit at Vancouver General Hospital. During this period, I devoted all of my days to being with her at the hospital. Nestled sixteen floors above the city bustle, we enjoyed one another's company. Either she would lie in bed while I sat in a chair next to her, or we'd be together on the outside deck, my grandma sitting in her wheelchair in her bright pink bathrobe.

We talked about everything and nothing. She told stories and I listened — not so different from the days when all of us kids were

The three generations at Zosia's home on Laurel Street, Vancouver.
Zosia is on the left, Barbara, the author, is on the right, and Danielle,
Zosia's granddaughter, who completed the memoir, is in the centre, 2001.

little and we sat around the kitchen table at her house on Laurel
Street, snacking on candies and chips while Grandma told us
about her childhood, her family and her escape from Warsaw.

Grandma and I talked a lot about my mother, and I asked her
about an incident that had troubled me for a long time: when she

found my mom crying in the basement during that first Sunday dinner at her house after my parents' separation, and sternly told her to stop.

My mother recounted this story to me a few months later, adding how hurt and angry Grandma's dismissive reaction had made her. I remember thinking how often Mom's dismissiveness had left me feeling hurt and angry. I had never tried to explain this to my mother, and she had an equally difficult time trying to express her feelings to her mother. Now, sitting with Grandma in her hospital room, I wanted to break the silence that had become so ingrained in our family. So I asked her directly, "Grandma, how could you have been so insensitive to Mom's feelings that night?"

My grandmother responded with such clarity, it was as though the conversation with Mom had happened the night before. "I told Barbie to stop crying because I knew there was no reason for her to cry," she said. "She needed to accept that your dad didn't love her any more and move on."

The brutal honesty in my grandmother's words was hard to hear, even after five years. "But Grandma," I said, "don't you realize that it isn't as easy as just accepting somebody doesn't love you any more and then moving on? Mom was in pain and she needed your love and support."

"I know she did," my grandmother answered. "And it was awful to see her so upset. But I also know that we just have to keep pushing forward when life is hard. That is how we survive."

About the Author

BARBARA BLUMAN was a respected Vancouver lawyer and one of B.C.'s first female arbitrators. An independent thinker and feminist, she lovingly balanced raising her three children with her career. Her commitment to human rights informed all of her pursuits. Barbara focused her law practice in the area of workers' compensation and served as a member of the Medical Services Commission, the Vancouver Public Library Board, the Board of the Contemporary Art Gallery, and the B.C. Paramedics Licensing Board. Her deep commitment to Holocaust understanding and her passion for writing inspired her to write the story of her mother's life in Poland and her journey from Warsaw to Vancouver during the Holocaust. Barbara was diagnosed with terminal cancer mid-project and died in 2001. Her daughter Danielle assembled her mother's papers and worked with Ronsdale Press and the Vancouver Holocaust Education Centre to ensure that the book was published.

Marquis Book Printing Inc.

Québec, Canada
2009